HOW WOULD YOU SURVIVE IN THE
MIDDLE AGES?

Written by
Fiona Macdonald

Illustrated by
Mark Peppé

Created & Designed by
David Salariya

FRANKLIN WATTS
A Division of Grolier Publishing

NEW YORK • LONDON • HONG KONG • SYDNEY
DANBURY, CONNECTICUT

David Salariya — *Director*
Penny Clarke — *Editor*
Dr. Tom Williamson — *Consultant*

DAVID SALARIYA

was born in Dundee, Scotland, where he studied illustration and printmaking. He has illustrated a wide range of books on botanical, historical, and mythical subjects. He has created and designed many new series of books for publishers worldwide. In 1989 he established the Salariya Book Company. He lives in England with his wife, the illustrator Shirley Willis.

FIONA MACDONALD

studied history at Cambridge University and at the University of East Anglia, where she is a part-time tutor in medieval history. She also taught in schools and is the author of numerous books for children on historical topics, including **Cities**, in the *Timelines* series.

MARK PEPPÉ

studied painting and etching at the Slade School, London. He has been a freelance illustrator since 1962 and has also taught illustration at Eastbourne College of Art. He is a major contributor to the *Timelines* and *X-Ray Picture Book* series. He lives and works in East Sussex.

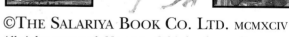

DR. TOM WILLIAMSON

studied history and archaeology at Cambridge University and is now lecturer in landscape history at the University of East Anglia. He has written many books and has appeared on radio and television.

Library of Congress Cataloging-in-Publication Data

Macdonald, Fiona.
　　How would you survive in the Middle Ages? / written by Fiona Macdonald; illustrated by Mark Peppé; created & designed by David Salariya.
　　p. cm. - (How would you survive?)
　　Includes index.
　　ISBN 0-531-114343-0 (lib. bdg.)　0-531-15306-1 (pbk.)
　　1. Civilization, Medieval – Juvenile literature. 2. Middle Ages – Juvenile literature.
　　[1. Civilization, Medieval. 2. Middle Ages.] I. Peppé, Mark, ill. II. Salariya, David.
　　III. Title. IV. Series.
CB351.M218 1995　　　　　　　　　95-3176
940.1 – dc20　　　　　　　　　　CIP　AC

First American Edition 1995 by FRANKLIN WATTS
A Division of Grolier Publishing
Sherman Turnpike
Danbury, CT 06816
First Paperback Edtion 1997

CONTENTS

BECOMING A MEDIEVAL EUROPEAN...

4 Time Spiral
Back to the Middle Ages

6 Basic Facts about Medieval Life

8 Your Map of the Medieval European World

10 Begin Your New Life Here

 14 YOUR HOME
WHERE WOULD YOU LIVE?

 16 YOUR FAMILY
WHO WOULD LIVE AND WORK WITH YOU?

 18 FARMING YOUR LAND
WHAT CROPS WOULD YOU GROW?

 20 YOUR FOOD
WHAT WOULD YOU EAT AND DRINK?

 22 YOUR CLOTHES
WHAT WOULD YOU WEAR?

 24 TOWNS AND TRADE
WHAT WOULD YOU MAKE, BUY, AND SELL?

 26 TRAVEL
WHERE WOULD YOU GO?

 28 SPORTS AND GAMES
HOW WOULD YOU HAVE FUN?

 30 GOVERNMENT
WHICH LAWS RULED YOUR LIFE?

 32 KNIGHTS AND CASTLES
WHO WERE YOUR ENEMIES?

 34 SICKNESS AND HEALTH
WHAT HAPPENED WHEN YOU FELT ILL?

 36 GOD AND THE CHURCH
WHAT WOULD YOU BELIEVE IN?

 38 SCHOOLS AND SCHOLARS
WHAT WOULD YOU LEARN?

 40 YOUR HISTORY
HOW WOULD YOU RECORD YOUR TIMES?

42 How Do We Know?

44 Timespan

45 Have You Survived?

46 Glossary

48 Index

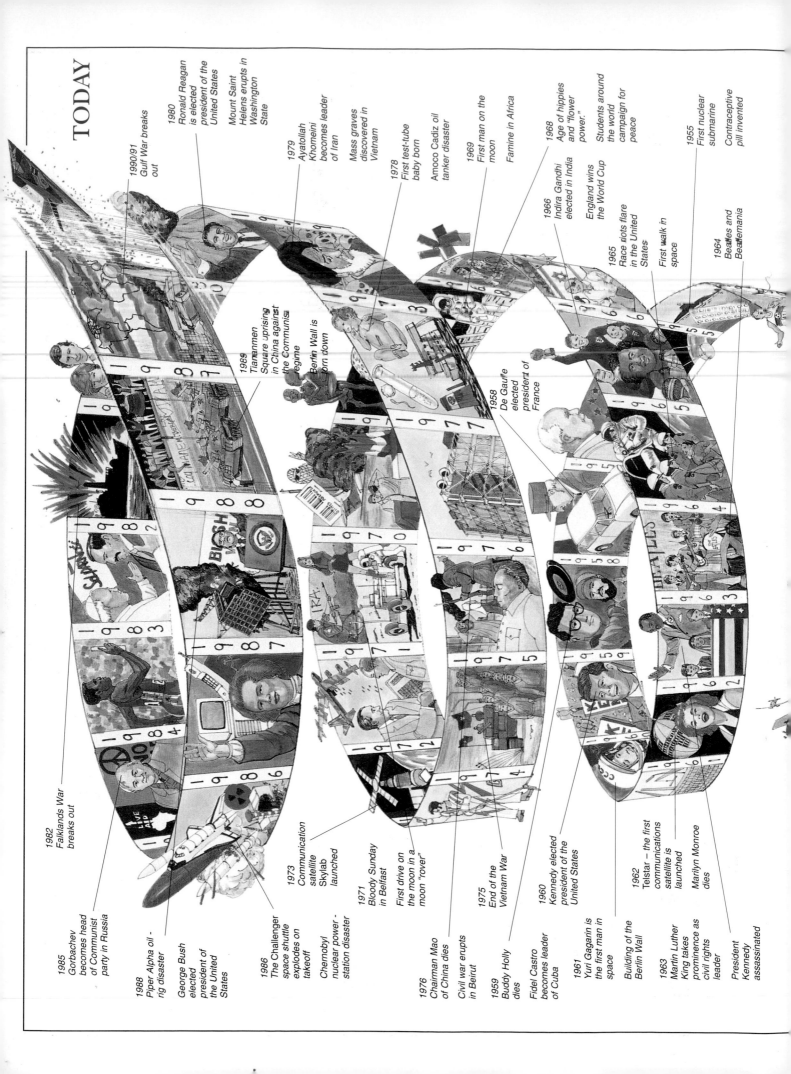

TODAY

1990/91
Gulf War breaks out

1980
Ronald Reagan is elected president of the United States

Mount Saint Helens erupts in Washington State

1979
Ayatollah Khomeini becomes leader of Iran

Mass graves discovered in Vietnam

1978
First test-tube baby born

Amoco Cadiz oil tanker disaster

1969
First man on the moon

Famine in Africa

1968
Age of hippies and "flower power."

Students around the world campaign for peace

1966
Indira Gandhi elected in India

England wins the World Cup

1965
Race riots flare in the United States

First walk in space

1955
First nuclear submarine

Contraceptive pill invented

1989
Tiananmen Square uprising in China against the Communist regime

Berlin Wall is torn down

1964
Beatles and Beatlemania

1958
De Gaulle elected president of France

1982
Falklands War breaks out

1973
Communication satellite Skylab launched

1971
Bloody Sunday in Belfast

First drive on the moon in a moon "rover"

1975
End of the Vietnam War

1960
Kennedy elected president of the United States

1962
Telstar – the first communications satellite is launched

Marilyn Monroe dies

1985
Gorbachev becomes head of Communist party in Russia

1988
Piper Alpha oil - rig disaster

George Bush elected president of the United States

1986
The Challenger space shuttle explodes on takeoff

Chernobyl nuclear power - station disaster

1976
Chairman Mao of China dies

Civil war erupts in Beirut

1959
Buddy Holly dies

Fidel Castro becomes leader of Cuba

1961
Yuri Gagarin is the first man in space

Building of the Berlin Wall

1963
Martin Luther King takes prominence as civil rights leader

President Kennedy assassinated

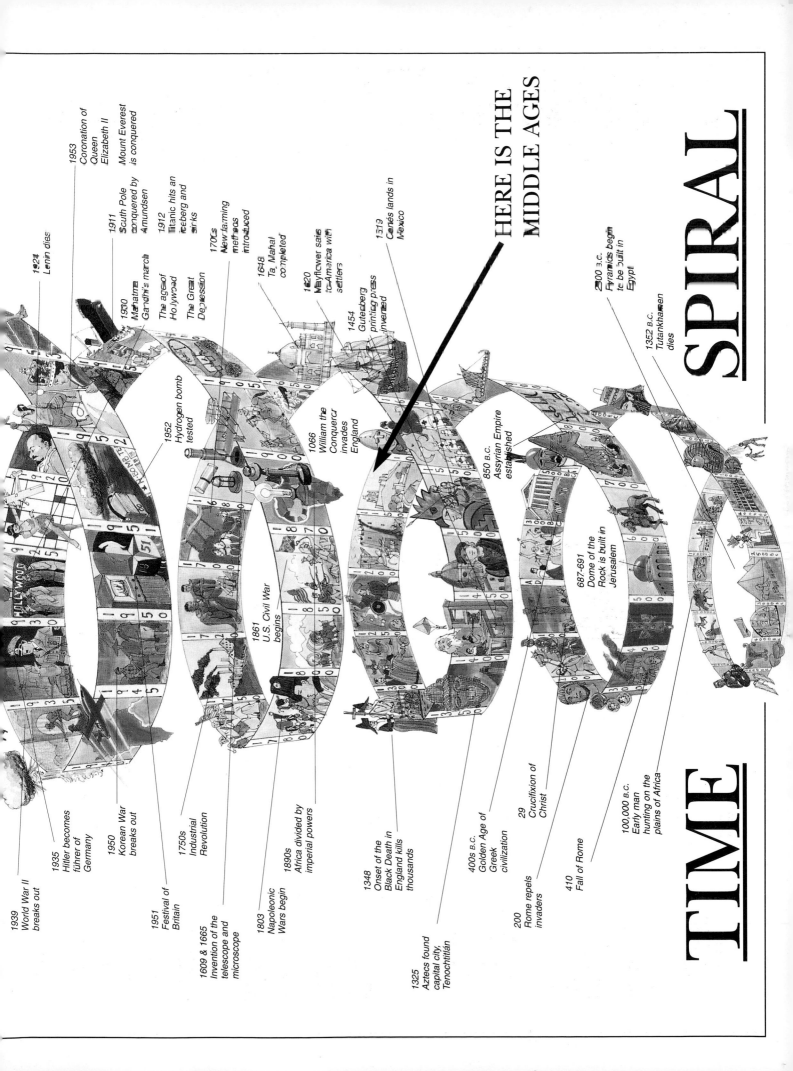

SPIRAL

TIME

HERE IS THE
MIDDLE AGES

1953
Coronation of
Queen
Elizabeth II

Mount Everest
is conquered

1911
South Pole
conquered by
Amundsen

1912
Titanic hits an
iceberg and
sinks

1924
Lenin dies

1930
Mahatma
Gandhi's march

The age of
Hollywood

The Great
Depression

1700s
New farming
methods
introduced

1648
Taj Mahal
completed

1620
Mayflower sails
to America with
settlers

1519
Cortés lands in
Mexico

1454
Gutenberg
printing press
invented

1952
Hydrogen bomb
tested

1066
William the
Conqueror
invades
England

850 B.C.
Assyrian Empire
established

2300 B.C.
Pyramids begin
to be built in
Egypt

1352 B.C.
Tutankhamen
dies

1861
U.S. Civil War
begins

687-691
Dome of the
Rock is built in
Jerusalem

1939
World War II
breaks out

1935
Hitler becomes
führer of
Germany

1950
Korean War
breaks out

1951
Festival of
Britain

1750s
Industrial
Revolution

1609 & 1665
Invention of the
telescope and
microscope

1803
Napoleonic
Wars begin

1890s
Africa divided by
imperial powers

1348
Onset of the
Black Death in
England kills
thousands

400s B.C.
Golden Age of
Greek
civilization

29
Crucifixion of
Christ

200
Rome repels
invaders

410
Fall of Rome

100,000 B.C.
Early man
hunting on the
plains of Africa

1325
Aztecs found
capital city,
Tenochtitlán

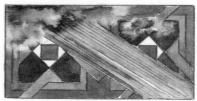

BASIC FACTS ABOUT MEDIEVAL LIFE

Homelands

COMPARED WITH present-day Europe, your homeland might seem rather empty. Towns were crowded, but much smaller than today. In 1250, Paris, the largest European city, had 160,000 inhabitants. Villages, high in the mountains or in the fertile lowland regions, were much smaller, too. The population of Europe in 1300 was probably 74 million, only 20 percent of what it is today.

Weather

LIKE THE EUROPEAN landscape, European weather was very varied. In Scandinavia and Russia, deep snow lay on the ground all winter; in Spain, Italy, and Greece, the summer sun could be baking hot. Throughout Europe, temperatures were probably a few degrees warmer than they are today. Around 1350, the weather grew cooler and a "little ice age" began. It lasted almost 300 years.

Wildlife & Plants

EUROPE WAS HOME to many more animals, birds, and wildflowers than we see today. Villages were surrounded by woods and commons, which formed ideal wildlife habitats. Vast forests sheltered bears, boars, wolves, and eagles. Chemical sprays had not yet been invented; this helped the environment, though fleas, flies, and poisonous plants sometimes caused serious illnesses.

Farming & Food

HOW YOU FARMED depended on where you lived. In cold northern parts of Russia and Scandinavia few crops would grow. People kept sheep and went hunting and fishing for their food. In warmer lands, wheat, peas, and grapes grew well. Farmers also kept cows and goats for milk. There were few machines. Plows were pulled by horses or oxen. Crops were harvested by hand.

Your Family

YOUR FAMILY was very important to you. Without their help, you would not survive if you became ill or old. Although religious leaders encouraged people to give to charity, there were no state hospitals or social services. Often, you worked alongside your family – boys helped their fathers in fields and workshops, and girls helped their mothers care for children and run the family home.

Lords & Manors

IF YOU WERE an ordinary peasant in the medieval countryside, your life would be controlled by the local lord. You had to work for him on his manor (big farm), or else pay him rent. In return, he let you have smaller plots of land to grow food for your family. Many lords had rights to enforce law and order on their lands. Some peasants were not even free to leave their lord's manor.

Craftwork

BACK IN MEDIEVAL times, you would find that there were very few machines. Apart from cloth produced on weaving looms, almost everything was made by hand. Craftworkers were very skilled. They learned their craft – anything from stone-carving or goldsmithing to saddlery, pottery, or embroidery – during a long apprenticeship. Only then could they set up workshops themselves.

Your Neighbors

IN A BUSY CITY or a quiet village, you saw a lot of your neighbors. You sold to and bought goods from them, and shared wells, streams, and grazing land. Without cars, medieval people walked or rode on horseback; all passersby could see and be seen. Houses had thin walls, so you could hear your neighbors, too. And anyone's behavior might be criticized at regular meetings of local courts.

Villages & Towns

TODAY, IN MANY parts of Europe, most people live in cities or towns. But when you travel back to the Middle Ages, you will find that almost everyone lived in the countryside, in small farming villages. Only merchants, lawyers, doctors, and craftworkers lived in towns. Medieval houses were built of local materials: stone and slate in the rocky hills; wood and thatch in the muddy lowlands.

Religions

MOST PEOPLE IN medieval Europe were Christians, but there were Jewish and Muslim minorities. King Edward I drove all the Jewish people out of England in 1290, but Jewish communities continued to thrive in many other lands. After around A.D. 800, the inhabitants of southern Spain became Muslims. There were also groups of pagan peoples in north-eastern Europe.

Languages

DURING THE Middle Ages, today's European languages were taking shape. They developed from four early "families": Latin-based (like Italian or French), Germanic (like German or Dutch), Celtic (spoken in Scotland, Ireland, Wales, and Brittany), and Slavonic (spoken in Russia and eastern Europe). Gradually, each nation's language became harder for foreigners to understand.

Your Name

CHRISTIANS named their babies after saints or people in the Bible; Jewish and Muslim people often chose names from the Old Testament or the Koran. Many babies were named after grandparents, or after rich, powerful friends. Parents hoped these "namesakes" would help their children. In many lands, surnames were not used, so people became known as "John the Smith" or "Mary the Baker."

YOUR MAP OF THE MEDIEVAL EUROPEAN WORLD

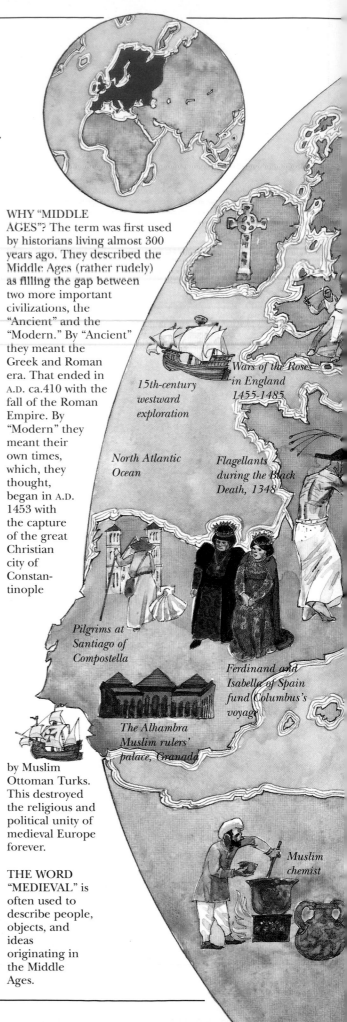

THE PICTURE MAP and the globe (right) will help you to find the places mentioned in this book. You will see that most of them are in Europe. During the Middle Ages, from around A.D. 1066 to A.D. 1453, a rich civilization developed there. It combined old pagan traditions – the heritage of Roman, Celtic, Germanic, Slav, and Viking cultures – with laws and customs based on the Christian faith and administered by strong, warlike kings. There were, naturally, many differences between the various European states, and these often led to war. But, when threatened with attack from outside, for example, from Mongol armies in the 13th century, European rulers forgot their quarrels. Encouraged by the Church, they joined to defend their shared traditions and way of life. Medieval Europe was only a small part of the world. Many skilled, learned, and powerful civilizations existed elsewhere, such as the Iroquois confederacy in North America, the Mayan and Aztec states in Middle America, Zimbabwe and Mali in Africa, the Vijayanagar empire in India, the Song kingdoms in China, the Muslim caliphate in the Middle East, and the Mongol dynasty in Central Asia. And, in spite of the vast distances involved, there were frequent contacts, for trade and scholarship, between many medieval lands.

CHRISTIAN CHURCH leaders taught that the Earth lay between two mysterious realms: Heaven (in the sky) and Hell (deep underground). After death, all good Christians would go to live with God and the angels in Heaven, while bad people would face eternal punishment from devils in Hell.

WHY "MIDDLE AGES"? The term was first used by historians living almost 300 years ago. They described the Middle Ages (rather rudely) as filling the gap between two more important civilizations, the "Ancient" and the "Modern." By "Ancient" they meant the Greek and Roman era. That ended in A.D. ca.410 with the fall of the Roman Empire. By "Modern" they meant their own times, which, they thought, began in A.D. 1453 with the capture of the great Christian city of Constantinople by Muslim Ottoman Turks. This destroyed the religious and political unity of medieval Europe forever.

THE WORD "MEDIEVAL" is often used to describe people, objects, and ideas originating in the Middle Ages.

15th-century westward exploration

Wars of the Roses in England 1455-1485

North Atlantic Ocean

Flagellants during the Black Death, 1348

Pilgrims at Santiago of Compostella

Ferdinand and Isabella of Spain fund Columbus's voyage

The Alhambra Muslim rulers' palace, Granada

Muslim chemist

SCANDINAVIA

By ca.1200 Christianity reaches Scandinavia

Baltic Sea

Alexander Nevsky (1236-1263) and rise of strong Slav kings

North Sea warship

Baltic trading ship

Crusades against pagan slav peoples

Moscow

Cathedral

Hanseatic trading league builds ports

Joan of Arc burned 1431

Gutenburg's Bible, 1468

Mainz

Timur (Tamerlane) leads new Mongol invasion, 1389

Limit of Mongols' invasion, 1242

Vienna

Great monastery at Cluny

Jan Hus burned, 1415

Slav kingdoms

Genoa

Venice

ITALY

Renaissance scholars and artists in Italy

Ottoman Turks conquer Serbia, 1389

Fall of Constantinople, 1453

The Black Death arrives in the Crimea, 1347

Mediterranean Sea

Constantinople

TURKEY

Crusader

Mohammed II, conqueror of Constantinople dies 1481

Crusader castle

Mediterranean galley

Ibn Khaldun, historian, 1332-1406

Saladin (1137-1193) leads Muslims against Crusaders

Jerusalem

AFRICA

BEGIN YOUR NEW LIFE HERE

WHAT IS this magnificent building? Why is it so big?
Go to pages 36-37

HERE AND ON the next two pages is a panorama of the medieval European world. It is not meant to be a true-to-life picture, for you would not find all these things happening so close together. It is meant to be your guide to this book. Start wherever you wish and follow the Q options.

WHAT IS this? Why is it here?
Go to pages 14-15

WHY COULD this ship be dangerous?
Go to pages 34-35

WHAT IS for sale in these shops down by the river?
Go to pages 24-25

A MYSTERY – WHAT ARE these people doing on stage? *Go to pages 24-25*

WHO LIVES in houses like these? *Go to pages 24-25*

HOW CAN this castle withstand attack? *Go to pages 32-33*

WHO GOVERNED this town? What laws did they make? How were offenders punished? *Go to pages 30-31*

WHO MIGHT be traveling in this horse litter? *Go to pages 26-27*

WAS THIS the best way to carry your baby through the streets? *Go to pages 26-27*

WHAT might
happen to you if
you disagreed
with the
Church?
Go to pages 36-37

WHAT IS this,
and why is
everyone so
afraid of it?
Go to pages 30-31

WHAT WAS life
like in this
monastery?
Go to pages 36-37

WHY SHOULD
you practice
your fighting
skills?
Go to pages 32-33

WHO WENT to
school here?
What did they
learn?
Go to pages 38-39

WHAT IS this
craftsman
making? How
did he learn his
skills?
Go to pages 24-25

WOULD YOU
be afraid of this
soldier?
Go to pages 32-33

WHY IS this
young man so
sad?
Go to pages 16-17

WHAT GAMES
did these
soldiers play off-
duty?
Go to pages 28-29

WHAT DID
medieval food
taste like?
Go to pages 20-21

WHAT DID
"ale wives" make?
Go to pages 20-21

WHICH CROP
are these men
harvesting?
What will it be
used for?
Go to pages 18-19

WHAT IS this
windmill for?
Go to pages 18-19

WHO IS the
lady of this
manor?
What are her
duties?
Go to pages 16-17

WHERE HAVE
these travelers
been?
Go to pages 26-27

YOUR HOME
WHERE WOULD YOU LIVE?

WHEN WE LOOK at splendid stone castles, tall timber-framed town houses, or pretty thatched cottages surviving from the Middle Ages, we might think how pleasant it must have been to live in a medieval home. But the medieval buildings we see today were a high-quality minority, designed for the rich. Ordinary houses have not survived. In fact, many peasants expected their homes to last only about 30 years.

What was it like inside one of these ordinary homes? Damp, drafty, smoky, and dark. Winds whistled through doors and shutters; mice and rats scuttled in the rafters overhead. Smoke from the open fire helped drive away flies from the stable, but it would have made your eyes sting and your throat feel sore. You would find the furniture uncomfortable, too – hard wooden stools, prickly straw mattresses, and rough woolen blankets.

WITHOUT gas, electricity, or oil, medieval people had to rely on wind- and water-power. Watermills were used to grind corn and to process woolen cloth.

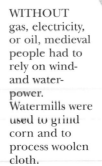

Local carpenters cut down forest trees to get wood to build your house. Oak is the best.

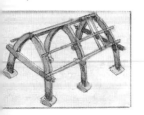

They use the tree trunks to make a strong timber frame. Curved tree trunks are used for "cruck frames."

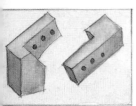

Carpenters carve precision joints like this to hold the frame together. Wooden pegs link the posts.

The walls between the timber posts are made of wattle (woven twigs) and daub (mud mixed with straw or horsehair).

Q

What other useful things – as well as timber – can you get from the woods?
Go to page 19

Stores of food

Clothes hooks

Trestle table

Fire

Stable

MEDIEVAL PEASANT houses often combined living space for ordinary families with stables for livestock. There was also space for stores of food to last all winter. Furniture was very simple.

Your thatched roof will be made of bundles of reeds from the riverbank, or layers of straw.

The thatch is held in place with sharp wooden pins, and with strong ties cut from hazel twigs.

The floor is made of beaten earth. Your house is often damp, since water seeps through.

Arrange a circle of stones on the floor to make a fireplace. Smoke drifts through the roof.

Ask the carpenter to make a door. If you can't afford an iron lock, he will make a wooden latch.

You will need wooden shutters for your drafty windows. Glass is too expensive.

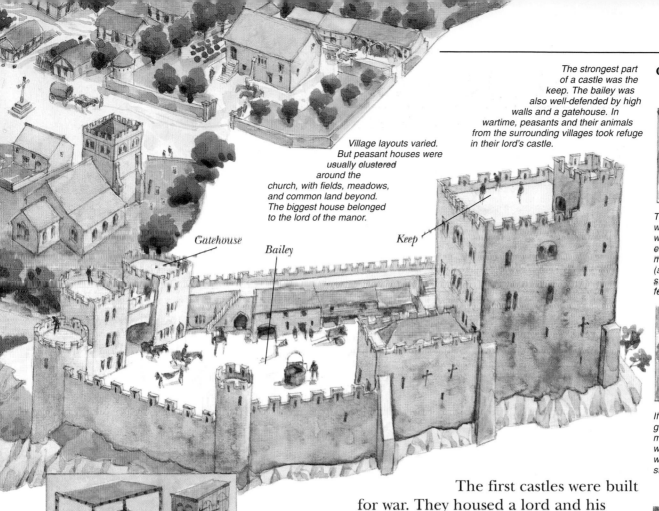

The strongest part of a castle was the keep. The bailey was also well-defended by high walls and a gatehouse. In wartime, peasants and their animals from the surrounding villages took refuge in their lord's castle.

Village layouts varied. But peasant houses were usually clustered around the church, with fields, meadows, and common land beyond. The biggest house belonged to the lord of the manor.

Gatehouse

Bailey

Keep

The first castles were simple: a wooden tower on an earth mound (a motte), a courtyard (a bailey) and a strong surrounding fence.

If a king or a lord grew richer and more powerful, he would rebuild his wooden castle in stone.

After around 1200, stone castles were built with "curtain" walls and lookout turrets to provide extra security.

Castle rooms were used as guard-houses and stores. There were also private "solars" for lords and ladies.

The first castles were built for war. They housed a lord and his knights, plus troops of soldiers. The noble's family had to live there, too. After about 1200, castles became more comfortable. Private rooms furnished with tapestries, quiet chapels, and flower gardens were added. In busy towns, space became scarce inside the walls. Houses were built taller, with rooms for shops underneath.

(Left) Four-poster bed with feather mattress and a carved canopy above. It was designed to be hung with curtains to provide extra warmth and privacy.

(Right) Aumbrey (cupboard) used to store valuable goods.

(Below) Cologne, an important German trading city.

BUILDING IN STONE

At the quarry, workers hammer wooden wedges into cracks in the stone to split it.

The stone blocks are then carried to horse-drawn carts, to be taken to the building site.

On site, masons cut and carve the stone into shapes following the architect's designs.

As a laborer, you mix mortar: lime, water, and sand. Mortar holds stone blocks together.

Or you might work the hoist – a pulley, rope and basket – used to lift the building stone.

When the stonework is finished, walls and ceilings are plastered and painted.

Q

In wartime, how would you try to make castle walls collapse?
Go to page 33

Daybreak: you get up, nurse crying baby, rake ashes from fireplace and light the fire.

Feed animals: corn for chickens, hay for oxen, scraps for pigs. Take drinking water to animals from ditch.

Children get up and put on outer clothes (they sleep in their smocks). Breakfast time: bread and weak ale or buttermilk.

Roll up straw mattress; sweep floor; put more wood on fire. Put dried peas on to cook pease pudding.

Q

On festival days and holidays, how would you relax after all your hard work?
Go to pages 28-29

YOUR FAMILY

WHO WOULD LIVE AND WORK WITH YOU?

WHETHER YOU were rich or poor, your family was very important to you. You relied on them for food, work, and shelter. Your family also gave you status. If your parents were nobles, you would be a noble; if your parents were peasants, you would be a peasant. It was rare for anyone to move up or down in society.

Because your family was so important for your survival, you were expected to be loyal. Sometimes, this meant hiding your real feelings and doing what your family wanted. For example, children were given to monasteries as a "gift" from their families to God. They were expected to spend their lives there. Adult family members had to try to win wealth and political advantages for their relatives.

Marriages took place at the church door. Couples usually exchanged vows (promises to each other to live as husband and wife) in front of witnesses. In medieval times, like today, weddings were celebrated with family parties.

NOBLE FAMILIES paid for fine works of art to commemorate dead family members, like these alabaster effigies of Sir Ralph Fitzherbert (died 1483) and his wife Elizabeth.

(Above) A "nuclear" family from northern Europe. Just two generations (parents and children) lived together. When children grew up, they left home to get married and start their own families. It was rare for parents to live with their grown-up children.

(Left) An "extended" family from southern Europe. Several generations lived together. Adult daughters left the family to marry, but adult sons remained at home. When they married, their wives moved in.

(Below) Kings and nobles kept magnificent "households" of loyal officials to provide food, comforts and entertainment, run castles and palaces, look after visitors, and help the king govern. By the 15th century, the king of England's household was over 500.

Fetch clean water from village well. It is very heavy to carry home. Meet other women and hear village news.

Work in cottage vegetable garden, to grow family's food. Some days, you have to work in the lord's fields instead.

Serve meal to family – pease pudding, bacon scraps and vegetables, with weak ale brewed by your neighbor.

Feed your baby when it cries. If you are working in the fields, your friends will breast-feed the baby for you.

Walk to nearby woods to look for firewood: there is no other way of heating your home.

Feed and milk cow; collect eggs. If you are poor, you may have only a sheep or a goat to provide a little milk.

Silver coronet, set with jewels and pearls, worn by Princess Margaret of York at her wedding in Burgundy in 1468.

"Poesy" engagement ring

Unless you were in the Church, to be unmarried in the Middle Ages was regarded as a disaster. A "good" marriage was crucial, for rich and poor. Noble families arranged marriages for their children while they were very young. (Girls could marry at 12 and boys at 14.) Parents believed that future prosperity, or the continuation of a noble title, were more important than love.

Peasant men and women were more likely to marry for love, but money, or land, was also a consideration. They also married later than nobles (in their twenties) because they had to save money to set up home first.

NOBLEWOMEN

As a noble lady, you have many duties. The most important is to give birth to a son to inherit your husband's land.

You entertain important visitors and help your husband in politics by being clever and charming.

Inside castles and manor houses separate suites of rooms were provided for noble ladies and their female servants. They were used as birth chambers and nurseries. Women spent peaceful days there, reading, sewing, playing music, and teaching their children.

You run a castle household and keep careful accounts. You manage your husband's lands while he is away.

"Courtly Love" was an elegant leisure style enjoyed by rich young noblemen and -women. They liked to spend their time listening to songs and reading poems about people falling in love.

Good manners, the latest fashions and delicate flirtation were all part of the game. Pleasure gardens with flowers and fountains, called "Gardens of Love," were built outside castle walls.

TOURNAMENTS were mock battles, played as sport by nobles and knights on horseback, armed with long lances, maces, and swords. Participants were often killed or injured.

As an old woman, you will win respect for dignified behavior and devotion to religion.

Q

As a noblewoman, your appearance displays your family's wealth. So what would you wear?

Go to pages 22-23

Spin woolen thread for weaving into cloth for family's clothes. You also sell to merchants from the towns.

Your children come home from work – scaring birds from crops. They are very muddy, and need to wash.

Family supper time: bread and soup. As a treat, the children roast apples on sticks by the fire.

It is dark. Time to get ready for bed – a big straw mattress. Everyone sleeps in one bed to try to keep warm.

Your son has torn his tunic – his only one. Light a rush taper and sit by the fire hoping there is enough light to sew.

Before going to bed, you lock the door and make sure the shutters are closed. There are thieves about at night.

FARMING YOUR LAND
WHAT CROPS WOULD YOU GROW?

January. You look after your sheep. The sheepfold protects them from hungry wolves.

IF YOU LIVED in the countryside during the Middle Ages – like over 80 percent of the population – you would spend much of your time working on the land. For many peasant men farm labor was a full-time job, and even country craftsmen – carpenters, thatchers, saddlers, blacksmiths, and wheelwrights – helped at harvest time.

The land where you worked probably did not belong to you. In many European countries, all land belonged to the king. But he could not defend it by himself, and so, in return for help in battle, he gave large estates (manors) to nobles who supported him. In turn, nobles gave some of their manors to knights, who went to war on their behalf.

These nobles and knights did not work as farmers. They made the peasants living on their manors work for up to 100 days in return for smaller plots of land to farm for themselves. Some peasants paid rent instead, and the lords used this to hire farm workers.

Strip
Strip
Strip

February. It is cold and wet outside. Your clothes can't really keep you dry. After work, you warm your feet by the fire.

March. Time to prune the vines on your lord's estate with a sharp knife. Then grapes will grow on the new shoots.

April. You pull up weeds growing among the crops. It's also time to gather herbs to make medicines.

Steward   *Reeve*   *Hayward*   *Bailiff*

Peasant   *Craftsman*

Manorial lords employed well-trained officials to run their estates and to supervise the peasants who farmed their fields or worked to maintain estate buildings. From the 13th century, officials kept detailed records of estate business.

King

Church   *Lords*

Knights

Peasants

Feudal landholding: In most of Europe land was held in return for performing services. Lords helped run the government; knights fought in wars; peasants worked their lords' lands. Gradually, these services were replaced by money rents.

Q

Who cared for you when you were sick?
Go to page 34

May. Prickly thistles are growing in the meadows and spoiling the grass.

You cut them down using forked sticks so you don't scratch your hands.

June and July. You cut the long meadow grass with scythes. Then you spread it

out to dry in the sunshine to make hay for the animals' winter food.

August and September. You harvest the corn and carry it to the barn.

If the harvest is poor there will be no bread next winter; people will starve.

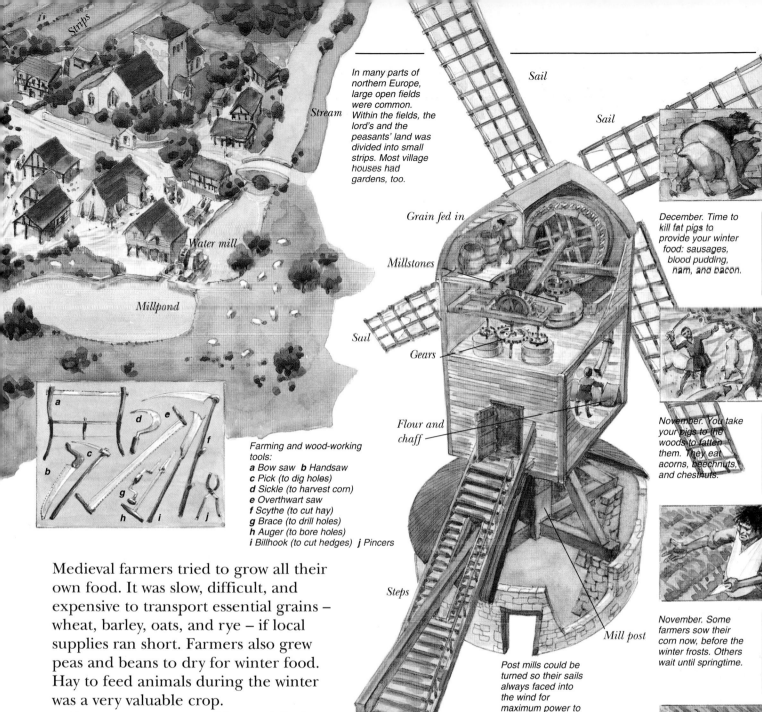

Strips

Stream

In many parts of northern Europe, large open fields were common. Within the fields, the lord's and the peasants' land was divided into small strips. Most village houses had gardens, too.

Sail

Sail

Water mill

Millpond

Grain fed in

Millstones

Sail

Gears

Flour and chaff

Steps

Mill post

Post mills could be turned so their sails always faced into the wind for maximum power to turn the millstones which ground grain into flour.

Farming and wood-working tools:
a Bow saw **b** Handsaw
c Pick (to dig holes)
d Sickle (to harvest corn)
e Overthwart saw
f Scythe (to cut hay)
g Brace (to drill holes)
h Auger (to bore holes)
i Billhook (to cut hedges) **j** Pincers

Medieval farmers tried to grow all their own food. It was slow, difficult, and expensive to transport essential grains – wheat, barley, oats, and rye – if local supplies ran short. Farmers also grew peas and beans to dry for winter food. Hay to feed animals during the winter was a very valuable crop.

Peasants grew vegetables and fruits – peas, cherries, quinces – in their gardens, and kept chickens, pigs, and bees.

December. Time to kill fat pigs to provide your winter food: sausages, blood pudding, ham, and bacon.

November. You take your pigs to the woods to fatten them. They eat acorns, beechnuts, and chestnuts.

November. Some farmers sow their corn now, before the winter frosts. Others wait until springtime.

November. On light soils, plowing is enough to prepare the ground before sowing corn; no need to harrow.

September. You watch the threshers hard at work. They use jointed sticks, called flails, to separate the grains of corn from the dry stalks.

October. The grapes are ripening in the autumn sun. You join the pickers and gather big bunches of grapes. They will be crushed and made into wine.

November. You plow the fields to bury the stubble left after harvest. Then you use a sharp-pointed harrow to break up clods of earth before sowing.

Q

What are your favorite foods?
Go to pages 20-21

YOUR FOOD
WHAT WOULD YOU EAT AND DRINK?

A typical rich recipe, "Birds Without Heads." Mix together onions, herbs, spices, eggs, and beef marrow. Cut slices of raw meat.

Shape the onion mixture into rolls. Lay a roll on each slice of meat. Roll up, so they look like headless, featherless birds.

Sprinkle the stuffed meat rolls with vinegar, sour grape juice, ginger, pepper, and cinnamon. Bake in a hot oven.

When the "birds" are cooked, decorate them with chopped hard-boiled egg yolk, so they look golden. Serve hot.

Q

Where could you buy spices to cook with, and where did they come from?
Go to page 24

IF YOU TRAVELED back to the Middle Ages, you might find medieval food boring and surprising. Boring, because most people ate the same sort of food every day. Compared with modern times, they had very little to choose from. Surprising, because medieval people who could afford it liked very strong, exciting tastes – sweet and sour, hot and spicy – that have disappeared from most European foods today.

Ordinary people got most of their nourishment from bread – an adult might eat a whole large loaf at a meal. Peasant bread was dark brown, coarse, and gritty. The grit came from millstones used to grind the grain into flour. It ground down teeth, too. Thick pottage – a soupy stew – was a common dish, made with peas or beans, vegetables, and bones. Extra flavor was added with pepper, garlic, and herbs. Meat, eggs, and cheese were luxuries, eaten on special occasions. Peasants drank weak ale, brewed by village "ale wives."

(Above) Castles and manor houses had large kitchens, where food was cooked for the lord's family and servants. Meat was roasted over a big open fire. Bread was baked in brick ovens.

(Below) In nobles' homes, meals were served with great ceremony by well-trained servants and pages, young boys from other noble families.

Strongly-flavored herbs were used to cover up the taste of stale or moldy foods that had been stored too long. Herbs with tough, leathery leaves, like thyme and sage, were dried and then crumbled and used in cooking. Delicate herbs, like parsley, were eaten raw. Flowers were eaten in salads.

Borage

Primrose

Parsley

Sweet Violet

MAKING WINE

Pick grapes when they are ripe. Unripe grapes are no good for wine-making. Use them to make sour grape juice (like vinegar). Sort your grapes and throw rotten ones away. Unless you are an expert, they will turn your wine bad.

Tip your grapes into a big wooden vat. Then jump up and down on them, to crush them and release the juice.

Add yeast to the juice, and put it in barrels to ferment. When wine is ready, pour into jugs, and serve with meals.

Unless you live in southern Italy or the Middle East where sugarcane grows, you will not have sugar to sweeten your food. If you are rich, you use honey instead. Perhaps this little bear, shown in a 15th-century French manuscript, was a pet.

Many families only had one cauldron to use as a cooking pot. With care, several dishes could be cooked at the same time: boiled meat, oatmeal puddings (tied in a cloth), and long sausages (chopped meat cased in pig's intestine).

Fishermen caught sea fish in nets. It was eaten fresh, or salted, or dried. Fish from ponds were also caught with nets.

(Below)
Bakers who sold moldy bread or short-weight loaves were punished by being pulled through the streets. People jeered or threw things at them.

What did you eat if you had no fire or oven? Many poor people lived on cold foods – mostly bread. In towns, you could buy hot pies, if you could afford them.

Meat was very expensive, so poor people turned to poaching, catching rabbits with nets.

Wealthy people and nobles ate finer food: stews, roasts, and sweet puddings made of milk, honey, eggs, and almonds. This rich diet was not healthy – it contained too much fatty meat and probably not enough bread or vegetables. But, unlike the peasants, nobles had no fear of starvation.

At feasts, food was finely decorated or made into a surprise. Live birds were (briefly) cooked in pies, and emerged unharmed to fly around the dining hall. At the end of the meal, there was a "subtlety" – an edible statue (maybe a ship, or a dragon) made of marzipan. Nobles drank wine, sometimes mixed with hot water and flavored with sugar and spice. Milk and cold water were not safe, cows might pass on diseases, and water might be polluted with sewage.

On market days, countrywomen walked miles into town to sell their eggs, butter, and cheese. Farmers drove animals to slaughter. The meat was sold by butchers in the market.

EVERYDAY FOOD

Ordinary people ate simple meals, such as vegetable soup with lentils. To make: take some dried lentils.

Put them in a big cauldron with chopped vegetables: try leeks, onion, garlic, and cabbage. Add lots of water.

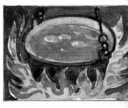

Cook over the fire for several hours. If you add ham bones or bacon rinds, they will improve the flavor.

Serve hot, with brown bread. If you can afford it, serve cheese and butter too. As usual, offer weak ale to drink.

KITCHEN WARE

  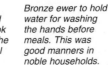  

You cook soups and stews in big iron cauldrons like this. They stand right in the middle of the fire.

A different kind of cauldron, designed to hang from a hook or a tripod above the fire by strong metal chain.

Bronze ewer to hold water for washing the hands before meals. This was good manners in noble households.

Kitchen knives from a 14th-century noble household. Diners brought their own knives to the table; there were no forks.

Pottery jugs like this were used for serving wine and ale in taverns. Medieval pottery was skillfully made. The jug on

the left was a popular type, known as a "bellarmine." It is decorated with the bearded face of a man.

Q

Who was the Master of the Grains? What did he do?
Go to page 35

YOUR CLOTHES
WHAT WOULD YOU WEAR?

WHAT ARE CLOTHES FOR? To cover us up? To keep us warm? To display our wealth and status? Or to show our sense of fashion? In the Middle Ages, like today, clothes served all these purposes. If you were a woman – especially a nun – the Church taught it was sinful to display your hair or your figure. These rules were relaxed for young girls and ignored by fashionable ladies. If you were a peasant – a man or a woman – you needed layers of thick woolen clothes to keep you warm. Men wore a tunic, breeches, hood, and cloak; women, a long kirtle, apron, kerchief, and cloak. Everyone wore woolen stockings or hose. Underwear was a baggy linen smock.

Rich people in towns, and nobles at the Royal Court, wore sumptuous clothes of silk, fine worsted, and velvet. During the later Middle Ages, these noble fashions changed rapidly; tight clothes, pointed shoes, and tall hats became very popular. "Sumptuary" laws were passed to stop ordinary people from dressing like this.

Peasant clothes remained simple throughout the Middle Ages. They were made of coarse homespun wool or linen and were designed for comfort while working. Clothes had to last for years; then they were cut down to make children's clothes, or given to beggars.

Priests, monks, and nuns, who had dedicated their lives to the Church, wore clothes that showed their special status. High-ranking priests, such as bishops, wore magnificent robes, but ordinary monks and nuns wore plain black, white, or brown clothing.

Fashions for wealthy people: Early medieval clothes were simple; late medieval fashions were very elaborate:
***a** English knight 1350*
***b** Spanish noble 1350*
***c** Italian noblewoman 1360*
***d** German noblewoman 1370*

***e** Italian townsman 1380*
***f** English noblewoman 1380*
***g** German page 1380*
***h** Burgundian noblewoman 1390*
***i** Burgundian townsman 1390*

***j** English clerk 1400*
***k** Young Italian nobleman 1400*
***l** Italian noblewoman 1410*
***m** English nobleman 1420*
***n** English noblewoman 1430*

MAKING CLOTH

First catch your sheep. Shear (cut off) its wool. Throw away any maggoty bits. Pick out the twigs and burrs.

Use stiff brushes made of teasels (plant seed heads) to untangle the wool. This is called carding, or combing.

Put wool on a distaff (stick). Pull out strands of wool and twist them between fingers and thumb to make thread.

If you live in a city on the cutting edge, your master may have a spinning wheel for you to use. It helps you spin faster.

Q

What other crafts might you be trained in?
Go to page 24

You could weave woolen cloth on a simple upright loom like this – but few people can afford to buy one.

If you were a craft-worker in Italy, Flanders, or England you'd use a complex loom to weave top-quality cloth.

Early medieval clothes were long and loose-fitting. Each long robe used several feet of cloth.

Clothes were sewn entirely by hand. It took many days to make one robe, so clothes were very expensive.

Hat with veil

Hair hidden in gold net

Hat with liripipe (long tail)

Neatly trimmed hair

Clean-shaven

Padded sleeves and shoulders

Bodice shaped with stiffening

Tightly-laced waist

Extra-wide skirt

Very short doublet

Clinging hose made of crosscut fabric

Fur-trimmed hem

Pointed shoes

Nobleman and noblewoman, dressed in the clothes worn at a royal court in France or Burgundy around 1430. Clothes like these were designed for display, not practicality. They were trimmed with gold wire, jewels, and fur. This made them heavy and awkward to move in. They were uncomfortably tight.

Getting dressed 1450. Underwear is a loose chemise (smock) and breeches, made of thin, fine linen.

His hose are two separate "legs" of woolen cloth. They will be tied to his upper garments with points (laces).

A codpiece (cloth pouch) covers the gap between the hose in front. On top goes a jerkin (sleeveless jacket).

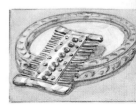

Round mirror made of polished metal, and double-sided comb carved from bone.

Three-part "gimmel" ring, with a design of two clasped hands enclosing a heart. Rings like these were given as love tokens.

A crucifix (cross) and rosary beads, made of gold and crystal. Each bead reminded worshipers to say a prayer.

Jewel casket made of fine, patterned leather. It is decorated with metal bands and an elaborate lock.

Women plucked out their eyebrows and shaved their hair to create a fashionable high forehead.

Men wore tightly laced doublets (short jackets) to give themselves small waists.

Men's shoes had long pointed toes. To avoid tripping, the toe tips were held up with chains.

Women wore extravagant hats; some resembled steeples, others had two "horns."

Young women wore low-cut, off-the-shoulder gowns. Church leaders condemned them.

Men wore short or shoulder-length hair, topped by hats with long tails and wide brims.

Q

What did you do when the preacher criticized your clothes? Go to page 37

EVERYDAY CRAFTS

As a potter, you would make bowls and jugs from clay and decorate them with a greenish-brown glaze.

If you were a cobbler, you would work with leather to make shoes, boots, belts, and bags.

If you trained as a blacksmith, you'd learn to make horse-shoes, nails, and iron tires for cartwheels.

It was hard to make a living as a knife grinder. You walked from town to town in search of work.

Q

If you wanted to learn to read and write, instead of learning a craft, who would teach you?
Go to pages 38-39

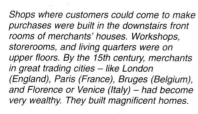

Shops where customers could come to make purchases were built in the downstairs front rooms of merchants' houses. Workshops, storerooms, and living quarters were on upper floors. By the 15th century, merchants in great trading cities – like London (England), Paris (France), Bruges (Belgium), and Florence or Venice (Italy) – had become very wealthy. They built magnificent homes.

In Venice, Arab merchants who traded with China and India sold precious silks, spices, and jewels.

There was no paper money in medieval Europe. Everyone used coins that were made by hand. First, gold and silver was cut into small pieces called blanks.

Next, the blanks were hammered with special punches, which made different patterns on either side of each coin. The edges were not ridged like modern coins.

It was tempting (and easy) to cut off tiny pieces of coin to build up your own hoard of gold and silver. Merchants checked the value of coins by weighing them in balances.

Apprentices with their master.

TOWNS AND TRADE

WHAT WOULD YOU MAKE, BUY, AND SELL?

Stone carvers made statues, fonts, and tombs for churches. They also carved doorways and windows for houses.

IF YOU LIVED in a town, what would your life be like? Dirty, noisy, crowded, smelly, and, probably, rather short. Disease spread very rapidly where lots of people lived close together without drains or clean water. Although there were a few splendid houses built by nobles and merchants, most ordinary families had to make do with just one room for working, eating, and sleeping.

On the other hand, towns were the place to make your fortune. Most town dwellers were poor, but a few "merchant princes," in Italy, Germany, and the Low Countries proved it was possible to become spectacularly rich, even from humble origins.

As an apprentice (top left), you spent seven years learning a craft. Later, you might become a master, making top-quality goods which sold at the highest prices to wealthy visitors to the town. Men and women making jewelry, embroidered silks, and beautiful dishes of silver or gold opened shops in London, Paris, Venice, and Rome.

Perhaps you would prefer to set up a business to cater to more down-to-earth needs: a mobile food stall, perhaps, or a bathhouse, or even a brothel? All were very profitable to run. If you were studious, you could train for one of the professions; doctors, apothecaries, lawyers, and scribes all had consulting rooms in big towns. There were bankers, money changers and money lenders, too. All charged high fees for their services.

Stained glass workers assembled beautiful windows using fragments of colored glass, which were joined by lead strips.

Skilled carpenters made fine furniture and paneling for rooms and decorated storage chests for churches and castles.

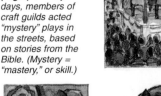

(Left) Cities and large towns elected leading citizens to govern them. Trade was regulated by craft guilds.

(Right) On holy days, members of craft guilds acted "mystery" plays in the streets, based on stories from the Bible. (Mystery = "mastery," or skill.)

Tapestry makers wove brightly colored pictures with woolen thread. They hung on walls and kept drafts out.

Glassblowers worked in Italy and the Middle East. They made fragile, precious objects.

Women embroiderers used silk and gold thread to produce beautiful robes for rulers.

Sculptors and carvers produced beautiful cups, caskets, and drinking horns out of ivory.

Men – and a few women – painted pictures to decorate churches, castles, and town houses.

Goldsmiths made jewelry for rich people and holy ornaments for churches.

Silk weavers wove magnificent fabrics, which were dyed using plants, sea snails, and minerals.

Q

What happened to towns in wartime?
Go to page 33

TRAVEL

WHERE WOULD YOU GO?

TRAVEL WAS difficult. Roads were dusty in summer and muddy in winter. In lowland country it took three or four days to ride 100 miles (160 km). Few people could afford horses; farm carts were bumpy and unsafe. If you lived on the coast, sea travel was quicker. But shipwrecks were common, and pirates lay in wait for ships out of sight of land. River travel was slow, and major rivers, like the Rhine and the Rhône, flowed through lawless borderlands. Travel on foot was even slower: 12 or 15 miles (19 or 24 km) a day if you were fit.

Pilgrims traveled on foot, on horseback, or by sea to say prayers and ask for blessings at holy shrines.

A pilgrimage had a serious purpose, but it could also be fun. Pilgrim groups traveled together for pleasant company.

Kings and queens, lords and ladies, traveled frequently between the castles they owned. They took servants, food, and furnishings with them.

(Below) Two medieval carry cots for babies.

Along the way, they stayed at pilgrim inns to rest and refresh themselves and to enjoy good food and wine.

Ladies traveled in litters (covered beds) carried by horses, or in lumbering wheeled carriages. Lords and their senior servants rode on horseback. Ordinary people walked.

(Left) Pilgrims bought cheap metal badges and bottles containing holy water as souvenirs to show they had visited saints' shrines

(Right) Medieval roads were full of potholes. Farm carts often got stuck on the mud.

Many great churches and cathedrals were built to house the relics of saints. They became popular pilgrim destinations.

Q

Were pilgrimages the only medieval vacations?
Go to page 28

At the shrine, the saint's relics (remains) were displayed in gold containers.

Pilgrims knelt in front of the relics and said prayers. They asked God to cure their illnesses.

Pilgrimages could be dangerous. Bandits lurked in woods and mountains, waiting to attack.

Pilgrims might be beaten and robbed – or even killed so they could not warn other travelers.

But most pilgrims returned home safely. They had exciting stories of all they had seen

Did going on pilgrimage help sick people get better? Medieval people believed it did.

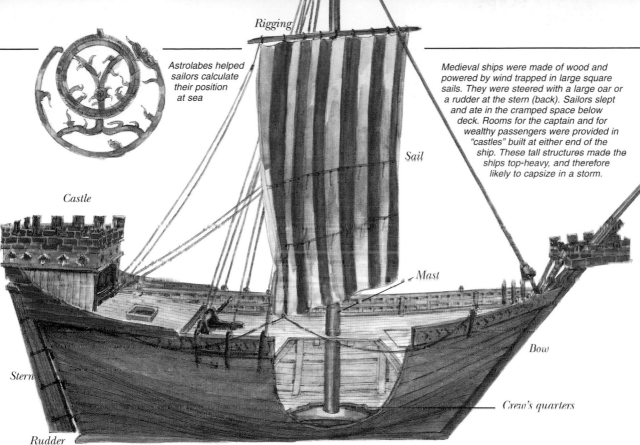

Astrolabes helped sailors calculate their position at sea

Rigging

Sail

Castle

Mast

Stern

Rudder

Bow

Crew's quarters

Medieval ships were made of wood and powered by wind trapped in large square sails. They were steered with a large oar or a rudder at the stern (back). Sailors slept and ate in the cramped space below deck. Rooms for the captain and for wealthy passengers were provided in "castles" built at either end of the ship. These tall structures made the ships top-heavy, and therefore likely to capsize in a storm.

Medieval carts could not carry bulky, heavy loads. These were instead transported by water on slow-moving barges.

Early medieval ships relied on oars to propel them through the water, as well as on wind trapped in their sails.

Later medieval ships relied mainly on wind power. As voyages became longer, oars were no longer practical.

Warships were built with "castles" at the prow (front) and stern (back). Soldiers stood there to shoot arrows at the enemy.

In spite of all these difficulties, travel was popular in medieval times. If you were a medieval traveler, why would you set off on a journey, and what destinations would you choose?

Most medieval journeys were short and unspectacular. Farm laborers and peasant women carried goods to market. Merchants made regular business trips to buy wool and cloth. Government officials carried messages from the king; justices traveled from town to town to hold courts. The roads were also full of wanderers: beggars, preachers, peddlers, minstrels – and lots of criminals.

Longer journeys were less common, more risky, but far more exciting. You might go on a pilgrimage, to trade in foreign lands, to accompany a royal visitor, or even off to war.

(Above) Part of the Gough Map of the British Isles, made in 1360. This section shows East Anglia. (East is at the top.)

(Below) Merchants like Marco Polo (1254-1324) crossed Central Asia to meet Chinese merchants.

MERCHANTS AND FAIRS

You're a merchant in a small medieval town. How do you find more customers and sell more goods? You go to fairs. You load up packhorses with the best local goods – wool, spices, jewelry – and set off.

Along the way, you meet other traveling traders: peddlers who sell small, cheap goods (pins, thread) and tinkers, who make and repair all kinds of household metalware – cooking pots, candlesticks, and knives.

Merchants, peddlers, and many other travelers met at great international fairs, held once or twice a year – at different seasons – all over Europe. Each fair lasted about a week; then it was time to pack up and move on.

Q

How might kings punish bandits who attacked travelers?
Go to page 31

SPORTS AND GAMES

HOW WOULD YOU HAVE FUN?

Acrobats leaped, danced, swallowed fire, and balanced on swordpoints to entertain the crowds.

Adults and children fought mock battles balanced on each others' shoulders.

Jesters were professional entertainers who worked at royal courts and at the houses of great nobles. Like comedians today, such men were sometimes criticized.

IT SOMETIMES seems that medieval life was grim, and full of suffering and hard work. But medieval men and women enjoyed more days off from their work than many people in Western Europe do today. There were fairs, festivals, carnivals, and processions all through the year. Officially, these celebrated great days in the Christian calendar, such as Christmas, Easter, and saints' days, but in fact they were often an excuse for a great deal of rather un-Christian wild, raucous behavior. Simple pleasures – dancing, eating, and drinking – were combined with ancient country traditions surviving from pre-Christian days.

Other excuses for having a good time included community fund-raising events, such as "church ales" (where food and drink was donated and sold at a profit to pay for something like church repairs) and feasts organized by religious guilds. There were traveling sideshows and fairs, and many professional entertainers. Villages might also hold sports competitions; games of soccer often became so violent that they were banned from village greens.

Popular children's games included stilt-walking and bowling hoops. Professional stilt-walkers, in fancy dress, took part in festival processions.

Contortionists and gymnasts twisted their bodies into all kinds of unlikely shapes.

At the end of the chase, the hunters kill the exhausted boar. They fling bits of boar meat to the excited hounds to calm them.

Many towns had public baths, run by women. Bathers sat in wooden tubs or took "showers" like this.

MUMMERS AND MUSICIANS

Traveling Punch and Judy showmen and -women set up their stalls at fairs and attracted an enthusiastic audience.

Q

Did peasant women get much rest on holidays?
Go to page 16

Mummers were ordinary people who disguised themselves with masks and fancy dress.

On festival days they danced and sang (often rudely) outside their friends' homes.

They also danced in the great halls of castles, to entertain the lords, ladies, and their guests.

They chanted rhymes and acted plays based on ancient pre-Christian traditions.

Their animal masks represented wild forces of nature which, people said, still existed.

Audiences gave the mummers food and money. If they didn't, the mummers might attack them.

BOXING AND wrestling contests were popular attractions at fairs and "church ales." There were few rules apart from winning. Spectators enjoyed betting on who would win. The Church authorities frowned on all forms of gambling, but there was little they could do to stop it.

Bear-baiting was a horribly cruel sport. Specially trained dogs attacked a chained and muzzled bear.

Chess reached Europe from the Middle East in the 11th century. It was popular with noblemen and -women.

There were taverns (pubs) and inns (hotels) in most towns. They served ale and sweet wine, along with simple food. Inns provided fodder and stabling for horses, and beds for travelers. Some inns were clean, others had beds full of fleas. Poor travelers slept on straw mattresses next to strangers. Rich travelers paid for private rooms.

In taverns, ordinary men – and sometimes women – played dice. They also made bets on which numbers they could throw.

Other people bet on horse races, wrestling matches, and cockfights. Cockfights were cruel, but very popular.

Playing cards produced by the new invention of printing became fashionable among rich people in the 15th century.

People also enjoyed dancing on festival days. They danced on village greens and in churchyards.

Musical instruments included fiddles, nackers (small drums), trumpets, bagpipes, hurdy-gurdies (played by pressing keys and turning a handle), gitterns (guitars), and flutes.

Singers who sang songs of love and romance were always popular with the crowd.

There were ballads (songs which told a story) about such heroes as Robin Hood or brave kings.

There were comic songs, mocking proud nobles and lazy priests, and protest songs.

Q

Did medieval farmers care for their animals?
Go to pages 18-19

GOVERNMENT
WHICH LAWS RULED YOUR LIFE?

As king, what threats worried you most? Angry peasants armed with spades and pitchforks could be dangerous.

How would you feel if the knights – who helped you defend your lands – turned against you, and rebelled?

What would you do if Church leaders preached sermons saying you were a bad king who should not rule?

Could you survive if the lords and other nobles, who helped you run the government, stopped supporting you?

Q

What clothes would you wear at a royal court?
Go to page 23

KINGS, NOBLES, and Church leaders were at the top of medieval society. They were enormously rich and very powerful. Kings made laws, with advice from ministers and parliaments which were assemblies of nobles, knights, and leading citizens who demanded the right to debate royal policies. Government officials, rich merchants, and lawyers also played an important part in politics, as members of law courts and town councils.

The Church made its own laws, and the pope appointed cardinals and bishops to administer Church business throughout Europe. There were often fierce arguments among popes, bishops, and kings.

Medieval society, around 1450: The richest and most powerful were at the top of society; the closer you were to the bottom of society, the more likely you were to be poor:

5 percent Kings, nobles, Church leaders
5 percent Wealthiest merchants, lawyers, officials
80 percent Poor, but managing: farmers, craftworkers, servants
10 percent Very poor: old people, widows, people unable to work

Kings were crowned at elaborate ceremonies which included prayers, psalms, and anointing (marking with holy oil). Usually, the Church supported royal power. After being crowned, the king sat on his throne and was given an orb (jeweled globe) and a scepter (jeweled stick) to hold. Both were symbols of his power.

TRIAL BY ORDEAL

You are accused of a crime. This red-hot iron will show whether you are innocent or guilty. Hold it tightly.

Now your hand will be bandaged with a clean linen cloth and kept covered for several days. How does it feel?

The sheriff unwraps the bandages and inspects your hand. If the burn is healing, you are innocent.

If the burn is not healing, it means God has sent a message to show you are guilty. You will be executed.

Trial by combat was a different kind of ordeal. The accuser and the person he accused fought each other.

If you won, it showed you were innocent. God had helped you win. If you lost the fight you were guilty.

Most people in medieval society were poor and powerless. As an ordinary person, you had few possessions, meager savings, and no job security. You usually could not afford to fight for your rights in royal law courts and faced severe punishments if you rioted or rebelled. In good years, you managed to achieve a moderately comfortable standard of living, but you could easily fall into poverty through bad harvests, accidents, or illness.

If you were a poor person, you almost certainly would fear the powerful people who governed your country. But you might not respect them. Many medieval complaints and criticism survive

KING EDWARD'S LAWS

King Edward I of England (1239-1307) fought against crime. He appointed village constables to keep law and order.

Kings made laws, with advice from parliaments and appointed judges. People accused of crimes were brought before royal courts in chains. Scribes kept records of court proceedings.

Gangs of criminals hid in wild areas, ready to attack travelers or raid villages nearby.

Before people could hold land from a lord, they had to do homage (a ceremony showing respect and promising obedience) to him. Great nobles did homage to the king.

He made new laws and created a team of magistrates (local judges) called justices of the peace.

Local lords, or their stewards, held courts for their tenants several times a year. All tenants had to attend. Tenants who refused to pay rent to the lord or to work for him were fined. These courts also heard disputes about petty crimes – such as slander or animals straying into the crops – and about peasants' right to hold land from the lord.

Poor people were seen as a problem in medieval society, especially in towns. They went there hoping to find work or to receive free food from rich townspeople or from monasteries and nunneries. But local councils thought they would steal, cause riots or spread disease. In times of famine, armed troops drove crowds of poor people out of cities like Florence, Italy.

He gave orders to cut down trees and bushes beside the main roads, so bandits would have nowhere to hide.

The death penalty was introduced for many small-scale crimes, such as stealing livestock and burglary.

PUNISHMENTS

If you were found guilty, you might be punished in several ways. You could be put in the stocks.

You might be locked in prison. It was cold, damp, and dirty, with rats and fleas. Your family had to feed you.

If you were rich – or if your crime was not very serious – you could pay a fine instead of going to prison.

If you had powerful friends, they could ask the king to pardon you – or they might bribe the jailer or the judge.

If your crime was serious, you would be sentenced to death. Nobles were beheaded: a bloody but quick punishment.

If you were an ordinary person, you would be hanged – a slow, cruel way to die. All executions were held in public.

Q

How did kings rely on knights?
Go to pages 32-33

Would you like to become a knight? This is what you have to do. First, be born a boy into a wealthy family.

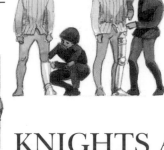

You'll be sent away from home when you are 8 years old to work as a page (serving boy) in a noble household.

You learn obedience and good manners. You are also trained to fight by soldiers in the noble's bodyguard.

You learn to use a sword, a lance, and a mace. You also learn how to ride a horse. It is hard work, but exciting.

KNIGHTS AND CASTLES
WHO WERE YOUR ENEMIES?

IF YOU WERE a soldier, what would your life be like? Would you match up to the descriptions of the perfect knight, found in medieval poems? He was brave, wise, handsome, and well-mannered. Daring and deadly on the battlefield, he preferred music and poetry at home. A sincere Christian, he was inspired by the love of a beautiful lady, and his motto was "Loyalty or death."

Of course, this ideal knight did not exist. But the poems describing his adventures tell us about the qualities – known as "chivalry" – that noble people admired in medieval times.

(Far left) Getting dressed for battle. (Left) 15th-century armor, made in Italy. German and Italian metalworkers were the best in Europe.

Visor closed

Chain-mail collar

Belt to carry sword and dagger

Pauldrons (shoulder guards)

Couters (elbow guards)

Chain-mail skirt

Cuisses (thigh guards)

Padded metal gauntlets

Poleyns (knee guards)

Greaves (shin guards)

Padded metal shoes

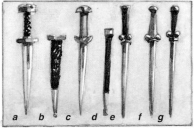

(a-d) Daggers (with sheaths), from 15th-century Germany. (e-g) Long knives, worn from a looped belt, English.

Knights practiced fighting with swords to increase their strength and speed in battle.

When you are about 14, you will go to the army camp with your lord and help him, acting as his squire.

You will also learn how to run a tournament – a glamorous mock battle with rich prizes for winners.

When the king says you are ready to become a knight, you prepare carefully. You spend all night in church, praying.

You have a bath, not because you are dirty – pages were taught to be clean – but to symbolize your fresh start in life.

You kneel before the king and promise to be obedient and loyal. He touches you on the shoulders with his sword.

The king then says, "Arise, Sir Knight," and presents you with a sword. At long last, you are a knight.

During tournaments, fully armed knights, mounted on armored horses, charged at one another in the "lists" (an arena with a barrier down the middle), trying to unseat each other. Knights wore fantastically decorated helmets, often showing their family crest. They might also attach a glove or a ribbon given to them by a lady.

A FIGHTING CHANCE

Before the battle, your leader makes a rousing speech. He says that God is with you and you are sure to win.

In wartime, life for knights and ordinary soldiers was very different from the elegant existence imagined by poets. Tactics were crude but effective: smash the enemy with whatever weapons you can. On the battlefield, heavily armored knights charged at ranks of foot-soldiers, spearing them with lances or slashing them with swords. Meanwhile, the enemy replied with a hail of arrows, or, after around 1320, lethal cross-bow bolts.

When attacking a city or a castle, armies tried to force a way through the walls with siege engines, or they simply surrounded the place and waited while the inhabitants starved to death.

The fighting is horrible, you are terrified. You see many of your friends wounded or killed. You fight to survive.

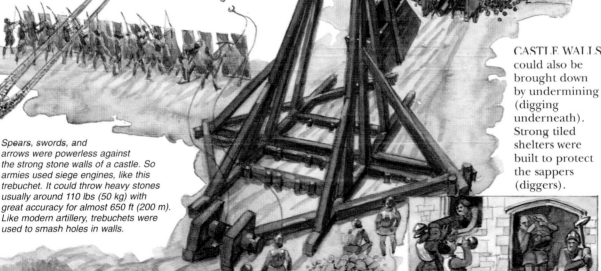

Spears, swords, and arrows were powerless against the strong stone walls of a castle. So armies used siege engines, like this trebuchet. It could throw heavy stones usually around 110 lbs (50 kg) with great accuracy for almost 650 ft (200 m). Like modern artillery, trebuchets were used to smash holes in walls.

CASTLE WALLS could also be brought down by undermining (digging underneath). Strong tiled shelters were built to protect the sappers (diggers).

Bad luck. You stayed alive during the battle, but you have been captured by the enemy. Now you wait in prison.

Victorious soldiers looted castles, towns, and villages. Troops also raped enemy women and killed old people and children.

You hope your friends will send money to ransom you. Outside your prison they have dug a pit to bury the dead.

CRUSADES

It is 1096. You hear a preacher calling all Christians to go and capture sacred sites in the Holy Land.

You think carefully and decide it is your duty to go. You vow to become a Crusader – a Christian fighter.

At a Crusaders' rally, you receive a cross-shaped badge, made of cloth. Your spouse sews it to your cloak.

You know that you may die on the journey or fighting in the Crusade. You settle your debts and make your will.

You say good-bye to your family. This makes you sad; you will be away for years and may never see them again.

You set off for the Holy Land; some Crusaders traveled overland, others by sea. Probably half of them died.

Q

What happened after you were dead?
Go to page 37

You feel your strength is failing. You must make a will, to say who will inherit your land and goods.

The Church says you must make a "good death." You confess your sins to a priest. He will ask God to forgive you.

You should bear pain calmly and be nice to the friends who sit by your bed. You tell them what you want at your funeral.

After the funeral service, your body will be buried. Your friends will hold a wake and say prayers for your soul.

Q

Why did your family order an elaborate tombstone?
Go to page 16

SICKNESS AND HEALTH

WHAT HAPPENED WHEN YOU FELT ILL?

Nuns and their servants cared for sick and elderly people in hundreds of hospitals all over Europe. Medical care was simple, but patients were kept clean and warm and given plenty of nourishing food. Space was limited, so patients often had to share beds.

LIFE IN THE MIDDLE AGES has been described as "nasty, brutish, and short." If you fell ill in medieval times, you may well have thought so, too. People probably had to endure much more pain and suffering than we do today. Although doctors, apothecaries, nuns, midwives, and wise women – as well as many housewives – tried their best to treat accidents and diseases, there were many illnesses that medieval medicine could not cure. Even so, life was not always much shorter. Many medieval people reached 70. But many others died when they were young. Almost half the babies born died from infectious diseases before they were five. Young women died in childbirth, and young men died in accidents or in war.

Medieval doctors were very learned, and medieval scholars knew a great deal about the human body and how it worked. But this did not always help the patient, because doctors and scholars also believed in many magical or "unscientific" medical theories – for example, that diseases were caused by the movements of the planets. They often based their treatments on these. Traditional herbal remedies concocted by village women were often just as effective.

Midwives helped mothers in childbirth. They were usually older women who had had several children. They were not trained, but had a great deal of experience, plus knowledge passed down over generations.

Many people became beggars because they were too ill to work, or because they had disabilities.

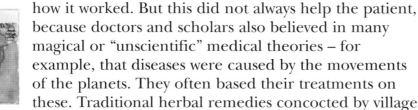

THE BLACK DEATH

The Black Death was a type of bubonic plague. It spread to Europe from Asia in the 1340s, carried by rats.

The rats carried plague bacteria in their blood. When fleas bits rats, they sucked up plague bacteria, too.

The rats bred and multiplied, and moved from ships to live in houses. There was food and warmth nearby.

There were also plenty of people for the fleas to bite. When they did, they passed on the bacteria.

The first signs of the plague were black boils (buboes), often in the armpit. Most people died within 48 hours.

Over 30 percent of Europe's population died. Plague victims were buried in deep pits. Leaving town was the only escape.

Leprosy was incurable and much feared. Lepers had to sound a warning bell or clappers if anyone came near.

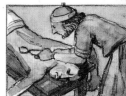

On the battlefield, doctors used strong iron pincers to remove spear tips and barbed arrowheads from wounds.

Diagram from a 15th-century medical textbook. It claimed to show which veins controlled the well-being of each part of the body, and which should be opened to "let" blood in an attempt to cure disease.

(Left) The Church stopped doctors from dissecting corpses so they could not learn how the body worked.

Many individuals gave generously to beggars and other needy people. Gradually, communities began to make regular collections of food or money for the poor. In Florence, Italy, the Master of the Grains organized regular gifts of bread for them.

Spectacles were probably invented during the 14th century. This is the first-known picture of them, from a French manuscript.

They bound broken legs with splints (strips of wood) to keep the bones straight while they healed.

To treat madness and severe headaches, they drilled holes in the skull. This was called "trepanning."

(Left) Doctors often "let" blood (deliberately made patients bleed). This killed or weakened many sick people.

(Above) Very few medieval houses had toilets. People used buckets or squatted behind hedges or in dark corners. Wealthy homes had toilets (called "garderobes" because the smell kept moths from clothes) but they were very simple: a seat over a hole, with a pit underneath. Castle toilets often emptied into the moat.

Doctors inspected samples of urine from patients. They said this helped in diagnosing many illnesses.

Q
What other subjects had doctors studied at a university?
Go to page 39

MEDIEVAL REMEDIES – DO NOT TRY THESE; THEY COULD BE DANGEROUS

Doctors also thought too much blood caused disease. Leeches (water slugs) were used to suck blood from patients.

Poultices (mixtures of bran, water, and mustard) were used to soothe inflamed joints and help cure infections.

Purges (strong laxatives made from herbs or figs) were used to try to drive sickness out of the body.

Soothing mixtures of herbs chopped up with honey were used to cure skin ulcers, sore throats, and stomachs.

Sick people asked priests, monks, and nuns to say prayers for them; nuns also ran hospitals and old peoples' homes.

Many people relied on "wise women" (or witches) to mix herbal medicines and chant magic spells to cure them.

GOD AND THE CHURCH

WHAT WOULD YOU BELIEVE IN?

On Plow Monday (early in January), plows were taken to church to be blessed at the start of the year's work.

Processions with candles on Candlemas (February 2) celebrate the belief that Jesus brought the light of God's message.

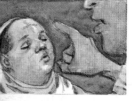

Ash Wednesday is the beginning of Lent (the 40 days before Easter). Priests marked ash crosses on peoples' foreheads.

Christians believe that about five weeks after rising from the dead, Jesus ascended into heaven, to be with God forever.

Q

How did you enjoy yourself on festival days?
Go to pages 28-29

IN MEDIEVAL TIMES, nobody believed that humans could survive the difficulties and dangers of life without help either from God or from mysterious, magical forces. Like everyone else, you would have held some sort of religious belief, however vague or superstitious.

The Catholic Church was the most powerful religious institution. It trained priests to perform services marking all stages of a person's life, from the cradle to the grave. Priests were also meant to give spiritual advice to their communities. Toward the end of the Middle Ages, there was widespread criticism of priests and church leaders for their love of luxury, their neglect of parish duties, and their involvement in politics. Scholars and a few independent-minded people began to demand reforms in Church teachings and to be allowed to study the Bible on their own.

In the Middle Ages many magnificent cathedrals were built in the cities of Europe. Architects and local leaders tried to build the grandest, most beautiful buildings to the glory of God and to increase the prestige of their cities.

The pope was head of the Church. He was elected by cardinals (top Church officials) in a secret ceremony. Although the Pope was a religious leader, many medieval popes played an important part in politics.

The Church punished anyone who challenged its teaching.

Rich people gave treasures like these to the Church, as thanks for blessings from God and to show their wealth.

In 1431 a French peasant girl, Joan of Arc, was burned as a heretic. She claimed to have seen visions from God. But she was also a political nuisance to the Pope and his allies.

The Church year can begin on Good Friday, Easter, Christmas, or March 25. Good Friday (two days before Easter) was the day Jesus died.

Easter Sunday (two days after Good Friday) is celebrated as the day Jesus rose from the dead. Easter falls on a different day each year, in March or April.

The Church teaches that on Whit Sunday (seven weeks after Easter) God sent his Holy Spirit to guide Christians. The Holy Spirit is often pictured as a white dove.

St. George, patron of England

St. Catherine, patron of girls who sewed

St. Christopher, patron of travelers

St. Lucy, believed to protect eyesight

St. Sebastian, patron of plague victims

(Left) Everyone prayed to the saints, hoping the saints would speak to God on their behalf.

(Below) Christians believed their souls would be judged after death. Good souls would go to heaven; wicked ones would go to hell. Paintings like this "Hell's mouth" were common in churches.

Christians also believe that Jesus's body is present in the church service called "mass." In June, Corpus Christi celebrates this.

There were many communities of monks and nuns. The first monasteries had been "spiritual powerhouses." But monks and nuns found it hard to keep up the original high standards, and monasteries declined. In the 13th century, new religious orders of friars were founded to teach the Christian faith.

There were other faiths in Europe, too. A brilliant Islamic civilization flourished in southern Spain. There were Jewish communities in many European towns – although the people were often cruelly persecuted. In the 14th century, there were still pagan communities in the remote northeast.

On Lammas Day, August 1, the first sheaf of corn to ripen in the fields was brought to the church to give thanks.

Michaelmas, on September 29, celebrated the end of harvest. A fat goose was roasted for a special meal.

HOW TO STAY OUT OF HELL

Confess your sins regularly to a priest. Try not to wear fashionable clothes.

Go to church often, and give generously to pay for new church buildings.

Study the Bible or, if you cannot read, listen carefully to preachers' sermons.

Help your neighbors; visit the sick; give to the poor.

Go on pilgrimages; fast (give up food); wear a hairshirt under your clothes.

Join rituals; these men are whipping themselves in sorrow for sins.

People believed that ghosts returned to earth at Halloween on October 31, the night before All Saints' Day.

Lady Day (March 25) is traditionally the day the Angel Gabriel told Mary that baby Jesus would be born. This is also known as the Annunciation.

Advent (the four weeks before Christmas) is a time of prayer and meditation in preparation for the joy and hope of Christmas.

Jesus was born on Christmas Day (December 25). In the Middle Ages this was celebrated with dances and songs: the first Christmas carols.

Q

What did the mummers do at Christmastime?
Go to page 28

SCHOOLS AND SCHOLARS
WHAT WOULD YOU LEARN?

I N THE MIDDLE AGES, what you learned and where you learned it would depend on the kind of family you were born into. Medieval people believed that education should train you to succeed in adult life – it was not something to be enjoyed in its own right. Therefore, a noble's child would need to learn completely different skills from a peasant's child. A merchant's child would learn something different from either of them. And, of course, girls needed to learn different skills from boys, since society expected them to fulfill different roles.

Mostly, you learned skills, manners, and the rules of good behavior from your family, although noble parents often employed tutors for their children; and merchants children, living in towns, might go to the local school.

Young boys, and occasionally girls, went to live with master-craftsmen's families. They helped in the workshop and learned new skills from day to day.

Very rarely, a boy might be apprenticed to an alchemist – a magical scientist.

First of all, you are taught to obey your parents. You should respect them because they are older and wiser.

If you come from a rich, noble family, you will be taught to read and write; you might go away to a school or university.

Your family's priest and steward will make sure you understand all the legal documents to do with your estate.

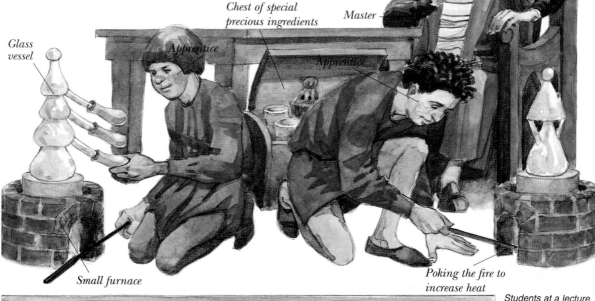

Chest of special precious ingredients

Master

Glass vessel

Apprentice

Apprentice

Small furnace

Poking the fire to increase heat

The priest will teach you about the Christian faith. If you are a younger son, you may choose to be a priest or monk.

Students at a lecture in 12th-century Italy. Italian universities were famous for medicine and law.

Q

Was it really glorious to be a knight?
Go to pages 32-33

You learn how to take part in noble sports – dancing, hunting, and hawking. This is politically useful; your family's friends run the country, and you want to stay on good terms with them by entertaining them at your manor house.

If you are born into a poor family, you will learn to work and to fight. It was important that all men and boys knew how to defend themselves – there was no national army. Nobles fought with swords, poor people used longbows.

You will have to help your father with all kinds of tasks, such as sweeping the workshop or stables. You should make yourself useful – running messages, fetching and carrying. There will be time for games after work.

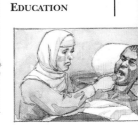

If you are a girl in a noble family you will learn how to run a huge household. You need to read and do math.

Your mother might teach you, or you might be taught by nuns. They also teach you about the Christian faith.

You might be sent to live in another noble household, to learn management skills from the great lady there.

You will also learn good manners, to dress well, to sing, dance, play music, be a good hostess, and do fine sewing.

You will be taught how to ride; hunting and hawking are very popular sports. You ride side-saddle.

You will learn how to run an estate while the lord is away, how to give orders and make people respect you.

You will learn nursing skills from watching skilled servants. You will also be taught to give to the poor.

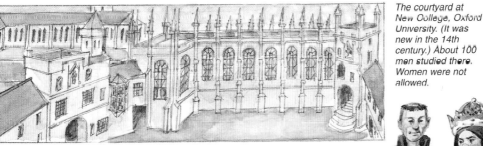

The courtyard at New College, Oxford University. (It was new in the 14th century.) About 100 men studied there. Women were not allowed.

University students had to take "minor orders" (the first steps to becoming a priest), but most became government officials or teachers instead.

You will learn how to manage the stock of valuable household linen and to care for the sick with home-made remedies.

(Below) Beautiful books, mostly on religion, were made by monks and nuns working as scribes in their monasteries and convents.

Authors presented copies of their books to rich and famous people. They hoped to be given money or valuable gifts in return.

Peasant girls living at home would learn how to work in the fields, raking hay and gathering corn at harvest time.

In the early Middle Ages, monasteries and nunneries were centers of learning, producing scholarly books, collecting wonderful libraries, and teaching young children. But schools and universities gradually replaced them. All university students studied a common curriculum: philosophy, grammar, linguistics, logic, mathematics, music, and astronomy. Law and medicine were extras.

If you were a peasant girl working as a servant you would spend your time cleaning and tidying up.

In a craftworker's family, you will learn your father's craft skills and will help with simple jobs. Most peasant men also need to know how to make repairs to their houses, furniture, and tools.

If you are born in the countryside you will learn how to look after farm animals. You will work as a shepherd or swineherd, watching over sheep and pigs while they graze. You will also learn how to care for farm horses.

You will be taught essential farming skills, such as how to cut hay with long scythes, or how to reap (cut) corn with curved sickles. The whole community works together to harvest these vital crops.

Q

What do you think kitchen maids thought about courtly love?
Go to page 17

If you came from a rich family, you ask the priest. If your family gave the Church a gift when you were born, he will remember that.

Did anything unusual – like a disaster or a new king being crowned – happen that year? Special events are easy to remember.

If you come from a noble family, your mother's secretary will have recorded your birth in the family documents.

YOUR HISTORY

HOW WOULD YOU RECORD YOUR TIMES?

MEDIEVAL PEOPLE were aware that they lived in uncertain times. Almost everybody would have seen friends or neighbors die or lose their fortunes suddenly, and for no obvious reason. Perhaps this is why medieval audiences were fond of stories about history. Reading about past disasters made their own troubles easier to bear.

But medieval history was not the same as the history we read today. Often, the historical topic was linked to a religious message: "Live a good life now, for who knows what tomorrow will bring." Sometimes, chroniclers were paid to write history with a political message, praising a king or a pope, and pouring scorn on his enemies. One 15th-century French writer, Christine de Pisan, wrote a history of famous women. She aimed to show that women were worthy of better treatment.

Poets and minstrels composed songs and ballads telling the stories of famous heroes – like King Henry V of England or Emperor Barbarossa of Germany – or of famous events, such as the Crusades. These ballads became very popular and were remembered for hundreds of years.

Clocks were rare – and extremely expensive – in the Middle Ages. They were originally designed to show the movements of the sun and planets, but they also told the time. This, one of the first ever made, was designed by the Italian Giovanni di Dondi, around 1348.

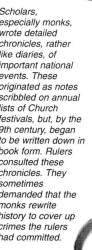

Scholars, especially monks, wrote detailed chronicles, rather like diaries, of important national events. These originated as notes scribbled on annual lists of Church festivals, but, by the 9th century, began to be written down in book form. Rulers consulted these chronicles. They sometimes demanded that the monks rewrite history to cover up crimes the rulers had committed.

MEASURING TIME

Q

Would you have liked to make a career in the Church?
Go to pages 36-37

Sundials show time passing – when it is sunny. The gnomon (central stick) casts a shadow on a dial marked in hours.

Candles show time passing when it is dark. They are divided into sections; each takes an hour to burn.

An hourglass is full of fine sand. It takes an hour for the sand to trickle from the top compartment to the bottom.

Bells tell you it is time for Church services – held at the same time each day. Their sound carries for miles.

You mark the changing seasons by noticing changes in wildlife; migrating swallows arrive in the spring.

Stars in the night sky also change with the seasons. You look for 12 special patterns – the signs of the zodiac.

At the beginning of the Middle Ages, documents were rare, and few people could write. From around 1200 onward, royal courts, government departments, Church officials, and manor stewards began to keep detailed records of their activities. They had many well trained scribes to help them.

Printing was unknown in Europe until the mid-15th century. In 1453, Johann Gutenberg (1396-1468) produced the first printed Bible on his movable-type printing press at Mainz, Germany, The first printed books were illustrated with hand-drawn designs. But soon pictures were printed from woodblocks.

MAKING PARCHMENT

Soak shorn sheepskins or goatskins in stale urine to soften them and loosen the hairs.

Take them out of the urine bath and scrape the hairs off, using a wooden stick. This is a very messy task.

Now stretch the scraped skins in a wooden frame and leave them to dry. This stops them from wrinkling.

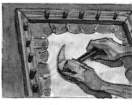

When they are dry, polish them with a padded wooden buffer. This makes a smooth surface to write on.

Q

What other products could be made from sheep and goats?
Go to pages 16 and 22

Printing on Gutenburg's new machine was still a slow, painstaking business. Each page contained 42 lines of text, and every single letter had to be carefully put in place by hand. It was easy to smudge the sheets of paper, too.

A 15th-century scholar. He has a desk, a bookcase, and book chest. Most scholars were men – women had few opportunities to study. But some did manage, for example, the nun Heloise (1101-1163) and the noblewoman Christine de Pisan (1364-1430), both from France. Books were valuable – it might take 100 days for a scribe to write one copy. To protect them, they were bound in leather-covered wood boards.

Place ink carefully over the type

These playing cards were printed in Switzerland in the early 16th century.

Forme with type

PRINTING

First, make little boxwood molds, each containing the hollowed-out shape of a letter. Pour in molten metal.

Leave it to cool and harden. Tip the piece of type out of the mold and make sure the letter is well formed.

Put several pieces of type together to make words. Work backwards, so your printed page will be the right way around.

Arrange all your backwards words in a wooden frame-work, called a forme. Make sure the lines of type are straight.

Carry the completed forme over to your printing press. Spread with ink, and place a sheet of paper of top.

Turn the screw of the printing press so that the paper is pressed down gently but firmly onto the inked forme.

Patterned ceramic tiles like this were used as flooring in important buildings like churches and cathedrals.

Pottery jug, made in Paris, France, during the 13th century. Its high-quality glaze and elaborate decoration suggest that it was used on special occasions only.

Mont-Saint-Michel, off the western coast of France. A medieval monastery settlement, built on a remote, easily defended site. It soon became a popular place of pilgrimage.

A 14th-century "pig snout" helmet, for a nobleman. It has a movable front section with holes for breathing and a narrow slit to see through.

This fine iron bolt, inscribed with "IHS" (a religious monogram) was once fixed to a door in 15th-century France.

Silver pennies minted during the reign of King Edward I of England (1272-1307).

An illustrated page from a 15th-century copy of an ancient Roman history book. Pictures like this are seldom accurate.

HOW DO WE KNOW?

HOW DO WE KNOW about life in the Middle Ages? An enormous number of objects and written records survive throughout Europe. But just looking at these objects or documents is not enough – although many of them are very beautiful. They also have to be interpreted, and, sometimes, restored or reconstructed as well.

Some types of objects are fairly easy to understand. For example, coins have survived in large numbers. Medieval arms and armor have been well preserved, too. They have been collected for their fine workmanship, but it is not difficult to tell why they were made.

Archaeologists can reconstruct pottery from fragments found in excavations. Pots can give us clues to the period in which a site was occupied and, perhaps, to trading contacts between producers and users.

There are individual buildings dating from the late medieval period in almost all parts of Europe, and a few complete late-medieval settlements too, such as Siena in Italy, or Carcassone in France. But they all contain additions or rebuildings from later centuries and should be studied with care.

Manuscripts, paintings, and all kinds of fine art also need to be studied cautiously. Medieval ideas about art were different from later ones – few artists tried to depict what life was really like. They were often more interested in using art to convey religious or philosophical ideas.

It is the same with medieval documents, from poetry to tax records. We must ask why they were produced before we can really understand them.

A fantastic creature drawn by a 14th-century scribe to illustrate a book of Psalms produced for the wealthy Luttrell family in England. Many medieval manuscripts are illustrated with imaginary creatures like this. They "grew" from the elaborate curving shapes of medieval handwriting.

Memorial brass to Sir John D'Abernon, who died in 1277. He is wearing armor. The lion at his feet shows that he fought in the wars.

The cathedral at Rheims, in northern France. One of the most famous and most beautiful medieval buildings. The west front, seen here, was designed by architect Bernard de Soissons and built between 1255-1290. **(Far right)** The Duchess of Suffolk died in 1475. She ordered a double statue on her tomb: this view of herself in splendid robes, plus a view of her diseased, dead body.

Computers help historians store and analyze data from historical documents such as tax records and manorial accounts. They can also help archaeologists make reconstructions based on fragments of medieval bone or timber.

Aerial photographs can reveal the outlines of medieval settlements. Remains of houses and trackways show up as lighter or darker green patches in growing crops because the soil is shallower (above houses) or compacted (trackways). Archaeologists have been able to find out about medieval people's height and state of health by studying excavated human remains.

TIMESPAN

1066 Duke William of Normandy invades England. English king Harold is killed in battle and William becomes king. The Norman conquerors introduce new laws and customs to England. Under their rule, the feudal system becomes more powerful. French is spoken by royalty and powerful nobles. English was not used at court until 14th century.

1095 Pope Urban II preaches a sermon calling for the first Crusade. Christian people from all over Europe go to fight against Muslims in the Holy Land.

1096 First Crusade begins. Fighting in Holy Land and elsewhere in Middle East continues on and off until 1453.

1099 Crusaders capture Jerusalem and set up a Christian kingdom.

1113 Paris becomes a great center of learning. Many universities founded between 1200 and 1500 all over Europe.

1130 King Roger II begins to rule over brilliant multicultural (Christians, Jews, Muslims) civilization in Sicily. He encourages Muslim scholars, the greatest geographers of the Middle Ages.

1160 Work begins on first cathedral to be built in new "Gothic" style in Laon, France.

1167 Italian ports of Venice and Genoa begin to develop as wealthy centers of international trade.

1187 Muslims troops led by great general, Saladin, recapture Jerusalem from Crusaders.

1210-1229 French government persecutes Cathar heretics. Thousands are killed.

1220 Mongols begin to advance toward Europe. By 1241 they have reached Hungary.

1236 Spanish Christian rulers capture great Muslim city of Cordoba, southern Spain.

1291 Collapse of Christian kingdom in Holy Land.

1307-1377 After religious and political disputes within the Church, pope leaves Rome and lives in Avignon (southern France).

1315-20 Widespread famine in Europe after harvests fail.

1337 Outbreak of Hundred Years' War between England and France (ends 1453).

1347-1350 Onset of the Black Death (plague), which will kill over one-third of Europe's population.

1378 Strikes by skilled craft-workers in wool trades in Italy.

1381 Peasants Revolt in England. Protesters demand better treatment by lords. Their slogan: "When Adam delved (dug the earth) and Eve span (spun wool), who was then the gentleman?"

1389 Ottoman Turks occupy Serbia. They capture Bosnia in 1463.

1396 Greek scholars at Italian universities inspire a new interest in the ancient Greek and Roman world. An artistic and intellectual movement develops: the Renaissance (rebirth) of learning.

1415 Portuguese sailors begin sailing west along the coast of Africa and into the Atlantic Ocean.

1415 Leading theologian Jan Hus, from Bohemia (in present-day Czech republic), burned as a heretic. Throughout the 15th century the Church persecutes critics.

1430 First cast-iron cannon built; guns soon replace siege engines.

1453 Turks take Constantinople.

HAVE YOU SURVIVED?

Q1 What would you do with some pottage?

A Use it to make bowls and dishes?
B Smear it all over your timber-framed walls?
C Eat it for supper?

Q2 As a lord, why might you find the peasants revolting?

A Because they didn't wash?
B Because they objected to the powers you had over them?
C Because they ate with their fingers?

Q3 How would you try to avoid catching the plague?

A Wear a magic ring?
B Stay inside your house?
C Get out of town as fast as you could?

Q4 Teasels were?

A An annoying game, played by children?
B Seed heads from plants, used in making cloth?
C Riddles that monks asked one another when they got bored copying manuscripts?

Q5 Why did knights at tournaments carry ladies' gloves in their helmets?

A As spares, in case they lost their own?
B As a love token?
C To stop the metal sections from rattling as they rode?

Q6 As a noblewoman, what was your most important duty?

A To entertain guests?
B To run the castle?
C To produce an heir?

Q7 Which was high fashion for women in the 15th century?

A Dreadlocks?
B Shaven foreheads?
C Ponytails?

Q8 Why would you be worried if your points snapped?

A Your cloak would fall off?
B Your shoes would come undone?
C Your hose would fall down?

Q9 Who were mummers?

A Women with children?
B Musicians and dancers who dressed up?
C Monks and nuns who chanted in church?

Q10 Mystery plays were:

A Medieval detective dramas?
B Plays you couldn't understand?
C Plays put on by masters of the local craft guilds?

Q11 Ash Wednesday was a time when:

A You cleaned out the fireplace?
B You sprinkled ashes in the garden, to keep out slugs?
C The priest marked your forehead with ashes, to show that you had asked God to forgive your sins?

Q12 A garderobe was?

A A lavatory?
B A bag to carry royal clothes?
C A well-dressed soldier?

To find out if you have survived in the Middle Ages, check the answers on page 48.

ALE WIVES women who brewed ale at home and sold it to other villagers.

APOPTHECARIES people who sold herbs, spices, and medical potions.

APPRENTICE young boy or girl living in a craftworker's family and being trained in craft skills.

BAILEY area surrounding a castle keep enclosed by a strong fence or wall. Also used to describe the fence or wall itself.

BEECHNUTS seeds (like little nuts) produced by beech trees. Food for pigs; eaten by humans in times of food shortage.

BREWSTER a woman who brewed and sold ale.

BURGUNDY rich, powerful state, covering parts of present-day Belgium, Luxembourg, and eastern France.

CHIVALRY a brave, noble, courteous, and heroic way for knights and noblemen to behave, described by medieval poets. Few real-life men lived up to this image.

COMMONS open land close to villages, where peasants grazed their cows, sheep, and goats.

COURTLY LOVE a fashionable theory of how men and women should behave toward each other, described in songs, poems and stories enjoyed by young nobles.

CRUCK FRAME a strong wooden framework for a house, made of naturally curved tree trunks.

CRUSADES a series of wars for control of the Holy Land (see below) fought between Christian soldiers from Western Europe and Muslims from the Middle East between the 11th and 15th centuries.

DAUB a mixture of mud or clay, twigs, straw, and horsehair, used with wattle to fill the spaces between the wooden posts forming the walls of timber-framed houses.

EWER a jug for water.

EXTENDED FAMILY a family in which three or more generations – often including adult brothers and their wives – live together in the same household.

FEUDAL SYSTEM a system of land-holding and social control. All land belonged to the king, who granted estates (manors) to lords in return for their help in wars and their loyalty. Lords then granted smaller areas of land to peasants in return for farm work or rent. Lords also had a wide range of legal rights over the peasants on their manors.

FRIARS men dedicated to a religious life who traveled around, preaching the Christain faith. The main "orders" of friars were the Franciscans and the Dominicans, both founded in the 13th century.

GUILDS associations of craftworkers, which helped with training and provided quality control.

HERETIC someone who held religious views which differed from the teachings of the Church.

HOLY LAND the land where Jesus lived and taught; present-day Israel, Jordan, Syria, and Palestine.

JUSTICES judges.

KEEP strong central building of a castle.

KIRTLE a long robe worn by women.

LAW in the Middle Ages, there were three different systems of law operating in Europe: royal law (made by kings and administered by royal judges), local laws (based on ancient local traditions), and Church law (administered by the Church, and ruling religion, morals, and family life). Each kind of law had its own courts and officials.

LITTER a curtained bed, carried on poles. Used by noble ladies and invalids for traveling.

LOW COUNTRIES present-day Belgium, the Netherlands, and parts of northern France.

MAGISTRATES judges in local courts, who dealt with minor crimes.

MANOR a lord's estate (land plus various rights over the peasants there).

MONGOLS peoples from northeast Asia who conquered vast territories in Asia and the Middle East in the 13th and 14th centuries.

NUCLEAR FAMILY a family of just two generations – parents and children – living in the same household.

OTTOMAN Turkish ruling dynasty that conquered many Middle Eastern and Eastern European lands during the 15th and 16th centuries.

PEASANT someone of low social status who lives in the country and makes a living by farming a small plot of land. Most medieval peasants also had to work on their lord's estates.

PEASE PUDDING meal of cooked dried peas.

PILGRIMAGE journey made to a holy place.

POESY RING a ring engraved with words of love.

POTTAGE thick soup.

SHRINE a holy place (often a tomb) associated with a saint.

SIEGE ENGINES big machines to batter or hurl stones at castle defenses.

SMOCK a loose, baggy garment, like a collarless shirt. Often worn as underwear.

SOLAR a private room in a castle or manor house, used by noble families.

STOCKS a wooden bench with holes for necks, arms, or legs. As a punishment, criminals were locked into the stocks for several hours while people threw rubbish at them, or shouted abuse.

SUMPTUARY LAWS rules designed to stop ordinary people from wearing rich, fashionable clothes.

SURCOAT a sleeveless tunic, usually worn over armor.

TAPER a small candle.

TEASEL prickly seed head of a plant, used as a brush to produce a smooth surface on woolen cloth.

TENANT a person who occupies land or a house belonging to someone else, in return for paying rent or doing work.

TOURNAMENTS mock battles, often including elaborate ceremonies, fought between knights.

WATTLE woven twigs, used to fill the spaces between the posts forming the walls of timber-framed houses. The wattle was plastered with daub.

WROUGHT IRON iron shaped by a blacksmith into decorative shapes.

Page numbers in bold refer to illustrations.

A
Ale 16, 20, **21**, **29**
ale wives 20
apothecaries 25, 34
apprentices 7, 25, **38**
armor **32**, 42, **42**, 43

B
babies 16, 26, 34
bailey **15**
bakers **21**
bankers **25**
barges **27**
barley 19
beans 19, 20
beds/bedding 14, **15**, **16**, **17**, **29**
beggars 22, 27, **34**, 35
Belgium 24
Black Death, the **34**
blacksmiths 18, **24**
bread **16**, **17**, **18**, 20, **20**, 21, **21**
Bruges 24
Burgundy **17**, 23

C
carpenters **14**, 18, **25**
carts 26, **26**, **27**
castles 14, 15, **15**, **16**, **17**, 20, 25, **26**, 28, 33
Central Asia 8, 27
chess **29**
childbirth **17**, 34, **34**
children 16, **16**, 17, 22, 28, **34**, 39
chivalry 32
Christians 7, 8, 28, 32, 33, **36**, **37**, **38**, 39
Church, the 8, **15**, **17**, 22, 23, **25**, 30, **30**, 32,

34, **35**, 36, **36**, **37**, 40
cities 6, 7, **22**, 24, 33
cloth 7, 14, **17**, **22**, 27, **27**
clothes **16**, **17**, **18**, 22, **22**, 23, **23**, 33
cooking **16**, 20, **21**, 39
corn 14, 18, 19, **39**
councils 30, **31**
Courtly Love 17
courts 7, 27, 30, **31**, **31**
cows 6, **16**
craftworkers 7, 25, **25**, **38**, **39**
crops 6, 18, **18**, 19, **31**, 39
Crusades 33, 40

D
disease 25, **31**, 34, **35**
doctors 7, 25, 34, **34**, **35**

E
Edward I, King 7, **31**
education 38, **38**, 39, **39**
embroideries 7, **25**
England 7, **22**, **24**, **31**, **32**, **37**, **40**, 42
entertainers 28, **28**
Europe 6, 7, 8, **16**, **18**, 27, **27**, **29**, 30, **32**, **34**, **36**, 39

F
fairs **27**, 28
farmers/farming 6, 7, 18, **18**, 19, **19**
fields **16**, 18, 19
fires 14, **14**, **16**, **18**, 21
Florence 24, **31**, 35
flour 19, 20
food 6, **16**, **17**,

19, **19**, 20, **20**, 21, **21**, 25, **26**, **28**, **29**, 31, **34**, 35
France **23**, 41, 42, **42**, **43**
fruit 6, 19
furniture 14, **14**, **15**, 25, **26**, 39

G
games 28, **29**, **38**
gardens 14, **16**, **17**, 19
Germany 25, **32**, **40**, 41
glass **14**, **25**
God 16, 26, **30**, **33**, **34**, 36, **36**, **37**
goldsmiths 7, **25**
government 18, 27, 30, **30**, **39**, 41
grapes 7, **18**, **19**, **20**; see also wine
guilds **25**, 28

H
harvest 6, 18, **19**, 31, **39**
hay 16, **18**, 19, **39**
herbs 18, 20, **20**, 34, **35**
homage **31**
honey **20**, 21, **35**
horses 26, **26**, **29**, **32**, **33**, **39**
hospitals 6, **34**, **35**
houses 7, 14, **14**, **15**, 24, **25**, 39
hunting 28, **38**, **39**

I, J, K
illness 34, **34**, **35**
inns **29**
Italy 6, **20**, **22**, **24**, 25, **25**, 31, **32**, **35**, **38**, 42
jewelry **17**, 23, **25**, **25**, **27**
Jews 7, 37
judges 27
justices **31**

kings 7, **15**, 18,

19, **19**, 20, **20**, 21, **21**, 25, **26**, **28**, **29**, 31, **34**, 35
France **23**, 41,
France **23**, 41, 42, **42**, **43**
fruit 6, 19
furniture 14, **14**, **15**, 25, **26**, 39

25, **26**, 27, 30, **30**, 31, **32**, **40**, 42
knights 14, 18, **18**, **30**, 32, **32**, 33, **33**

L
languages 7
laws 22, **31**
lawyers 7, 25, 30
linen **22**, **23**, **39**
litters 26
London 24, 25
lords 6, 14, **18**, **19**, 20, 26, 28, **30**, **31**, **32**, see also nobles
love 17, **32**
Low Countries, the 25

M
magistrates **31**
manners **17**, **21**, **32**, 38, **39**
manor houses 20
manors 6, 18, **38**
markets 21, 27
marriage 17
meals **16**, **17**, 20, **20**, 21, **21**
meat 20, **20**, 21, **21**
merchants 7, **17**, **24**, 25, 27, **27**, 30, 38
Middle East 8, **20**, 25, **29**
midwives 34, **34**
mills 14, **19**
monasteries 15, **31**, 37, 39, **39**, **42**
Mongols 8
monks 22, **35**, 37, **39**, **40**
motte **15**
mummers 28
music/musicians **17**, **29**, 32, **39**
Muslims 7, 8

N
nobles 14, 16, **16**, **17**, 18, 20, 21, 22, 25, **28**, **29**, 30, **30**, **31**, 38, **38**, **40**, 42; see

also lords
nuns 22, 34, **34**, **35**, 37, **39**

P
packhorses 27
pages 20, 32
Paris 24, 25, **42**
parliaments 30, **31**
peas 16, 19, 20
peasants 6, 14, **15**, 17, 18, **18**, 19, 20, 21, 22, **30**, 38
peddlers 27, **27**
pigs 16, 19, **19**, **39**
pilgrims/pilgrimages 26, **27**, **42**
plague see Black Death
plowing 6, **19**, 37
poets/poetry **17**, 32, 33, **40**, 42
Polo, Marco 27
population 6, 18, **34**
potters/pottery 7, 21, **24**, 42, **42**
priests 22, **29**, 34, **35**, 36, **38**, **39**, 40
printing **29**, 41, **41**
punishments **21**, 30, **31**, 31

R
religion 7, 8, **17**; see also Christians, Church, monks, nuns
rents 6, 18, **18**, **31**
rivers 26
roads 26, 27
Rome 25
Russia 6, 7

S
saddlers 7, 18
saints 26, 28, **37**
scholars/scholarship 8, 34, 36, 38, 39, **39**, **40**, **41**

school 38, 39
scribes 25, **39**, 41, **41**
sheep 6, **18**, **22**, **39**
ships 26, 27
shoes 23, 24
shops 15, **24**, 25
shrines 26
shutters **14**, **17**
sieges 33, **33**
soldiers 14, **27**, **32**, **32**, **33**, **33**
Spain 6, 7, 37
spices **20**, 24, **27**
spinning **17**, 22
sports **17**, **27**, 28, **29**
starvation 18, **21**
stone carving 7, **25**
sugar 20

T
taverns **21**, **29**
tools 19, **39**
tournaments **17**, **32**, 33
towns 7, 14, 21, **25**, **25**, 27, **27**, 30
trade 8, **24**, 25, 27
transport 19, **27**
travel 26, 27

U, V, W
universities **38**, 39, **39**

vegetables 6, 19, 20, 21, **21**
Venice **24**, 25
villages 6, 7, 27

war 8, 14, **15**, 18, **18**, 27, **33**, **33**, 34
wattle and daub **14**
weapons **17**, **32**, 33, **33**, **38**
weaving 7, **17**, **22**, **25**
weddings 17
wheat 6, **19**
wine 19, **20**, 21, **21**, 26, **29**
wool **22**, 27, **27**

ANSWERS INDEX
HAVE YOU SURVIVED?

Here are the quiz answers, with pages to turn to if you need an explanation.

Count up your correct answers and find out what your survival rating is.

Q
1(C) – page 20
2(B) – page 30
3(C) – in fact medieval people tried all three, but only C worked; page 34
4(B) – page 22

5(B) – page 33
6(C) – page 17
7(B) – page 23
8(C) – page 23
9(B) – page 28
10(C) – page 25
11(C) – page 36
12(A) – page 35

10 – 12 Excellent! You will be rewarded by the king.
6 – 9 You will become a top churchman or make a successful marriage and run your husband's estates very profitably while he is away at the Crusades.
0 – 5 Oh dear! You're going to find life in the Middle Ages very difficult to survive!

ACKNOWLEDGMENTS
The Salariya Book Co Ltd would like to thank the following people for their assistance:
Sarah Ridley
Belinda Weber